PATHS OF
RIGHTEOUSNESS
IN PSALM 23

Paths of Righteousness in Psalm 23

A Devotional Study

Terry Atkinson

JANUS PUBLISHING COMPANY
London, England

First published in Great Britain 1994
by Janus Publishing Company
Duke House, 37 Duke Street
London W1M 5DF

Copyright © Terry Atkinson 1994

British Library Cataloguing-in-Publication Data.
A catalogue record for this book is available
from the British Library.

ISBN 1 85756 094 9

Cover design by David Murphy

Printed & bound in England by Antony Rowe Ltd,
Chippenham, Wiltshire.

Dedication

To my wife, Margaret, who has stood by me
in thick and thin – more thick than thin.

Contents

Foreword

No passage of Scripture has inspired more hymns, evoked more comments and embellished more occasions than this 'Shepherd Psalm'. Yet its spiritual force is not abated. Age cannot weary this ancient hymn; its influence will last as long as time.

So who can squeeze more juice out of this old-time hymn? The remarkable fact is that our author has done just that in this sparkling exposition. Colourful English, rich in abundant figures of speech, makes for exhilarating reading. There flow in quick succession a stream of vivid metaphors, lush similes, skilful play upon words, alliteration and assonance, producing prose which is a little heady at times, but always buoyant; and all in the service of the text set before us.

It is not to be read hurriedly lest you miss a pun, a word-picture or a verbal aside. Frequent references to other scriptures are luminous and interpretive, and the artful ploy of unusual phrases often takes the reader by surprise.

By inference, by indirect suggestion, by luminous phraseology the writer gives life to his comments. Grammatical pedants may be shocked by some of his verbal applications or unusual sentence-structure, but are the niceties of grammar the final arbiter of prose-energy?

'But does he faithfully expound this precious piece of Holy Writ?' you may ask. Yes, indeed! Every word is made to produce spiritual meaning. A light touch will often unlock a relevant parallel passage and help us see afresh some latent truth. His aphoristic style produces glowing gems of prose, his seemingly literary 'asides' bear illuminating thoughts. His anecdotes are pithy but pointed, his flashes of humour appealing. Echoes of other writers and speakers show him to be widely read. Above all, the personal appeal and application declare this psalm a guide to successful spiritual pilgrimage through this life to eternal glory.

I found these reflections refreshing to my spirit. I must read them again lest I miss the force of the apt allusions and spicy pleasantries that abound.

Aaron Linford
July 1993

Introduction

The Appeal and Wonder of Psalm 23

The most popular and famous part of all the Word of God is probably Psalm 23. Men have lived by it and they have also died by it. It has brought consolation to many thousands of people. The psalm seems to contain so much that is relevant in day-to-day living. It has ministered into so many situations. There is to be found in this poem sorrow and joy, righteousness and reward, coolness, stillness, oneness. In it there is no threat, no doctrinal error. There is also no mention of hell or judgement to come. The epigram paints its own picture of God and the believer. It could be, and has been accepted as, a Charter for any Church. It is at once a song, a psalm, a serenade. Every verse is almost like the strings of a harp and, as we read, we become the instrumentalist playing the songs of Zion.

There is no title to this psalm, nor is one necessary, for we can apply our own title according to the phase we are passing through at the time of meditating. Your name can be added to it. Every line, every verse, every statement is a title in itself. It comes immediately after Psalm 22 – which is the Psalm of the Cross – and leads on to Psalm 24 – the Psalm of the Crown. We have the Cross, the Crook and the Crown in these three psalms. They are music to our souls. Only after we have read the words, 'My God, my God, why has Thou forsaken me?' can we read, 'The Lord is my Shepherd . . . I will fear no evil, for You are with me . . .'

It is this psalm that was used at the coronation of Queen Elizabeth II. It is this psalm which is most requested to be read in sick room, in Church, or on parade. It takes its place regularly as the chief mourner at funerals, and the best man at weddings. When some have gone to the gallows or been burned at the stake, they have done so with these words ringing in their ears and its hopes abounding in their hearts.

Sinner and saint, rich or poor, high or low, pilgrim or peasant, prince or priest, foolish or wise – all seem to meet on this acre of God. All worship in this Church and bow before this altar.

When seeking help in time of need, when seeking light in darkness or healing for some inner wound, there is that in Psalm 23 which can touch and reach to the inner and hidden parts of life – parts too complex for human hands and ears to deal with. When the medicine bottle is empty and there seems no remedy for the pain then Psalm 23 is always there as a fulness. Not all who read it take something from it. We can read it without knowing the Shepherd and this minstrel of joy will never then come to life for us. The fingers will never move across the strings. It will be as cold as stone and as still as death, unless the Lord *is* my Shepherd. That Light which is in this requiem must first be in us. It will be, providing we make the Lord OUR Shepherd. We can only live in it, move in it and have our being in it as we surrender to the Shepherd.

The Psalm of David, this Kingly instrument, gives two recitals. It is divided into two scores. The first half deals with the Shepherd's relationship with the sheep. The second half takes us into the wonders of belonging to God – the feast, the oil, the table, the overflowing cup, the King's table, the King's house.

This sacred song is thought to have been written by David in the forest of Hareth (1 Sam. 22:5). Hareth means 'to plough, to engrave, to make a mark upon'. One can see why David needed the consolation of what was written. God, in that forest, was writing on David's soul. He was the tablet of clay, and God was using life with all its vicissitudes as a pen of iron. Some scholars feel it is the equivalent of Paul's Epistle to Philemon, written as he looks back over the years. David is looking back at the leadings of God during his lifetime and he wants to write a memorial for all who follow in his footsteps to read. He is bringing and breaking up his pastoral life in God and placing it into an ode.

An old legend has it that, one night as David lay asleep, the wind blew on his harp and the music was so sweet that he penned these words to that music from Heaven. It is meant to be sung and not just read. It is meant to be lived, not simply looked at and passed over. In life, as in death, there is nothing which knits the soul together so easily and readily, sowing contentment where it finds chaos.

Spurgeon called it 'The Pearl of Psalms' in one of his sermons. More than that, it is a casket of pearls. In every verse, word and expression there are hidden meanings, as nectar within the flowers. As the Acts of the Apostles is the outward manifestation of life in the Spirit for the believer, so Psalm 23 is the inner sanctuary of the heart. It is that inner revelation, inner understanding, inner throb and expression of life in Christ. 'Change and decay in all around I see, but Thou Who CHANGEST NOT abide with me.' Its years have not failed.

The Head of the Community or some representative of such would read this psalm whenever the family gathered together. It is not a war psalm, more a worship psalm. It was read when travelling on some long lonely journey. It was a bridge between 'God bless you' and 'Goodbye'. It is something of the heart rather than of the hand, a palm leaf rather than a sword. It is the hymn of the tranquil life expressing the great peace of all who love God's Law. It has influenced more people than gun, bomb, missile or bullet. Dictators, Kings, tyrants are mere titles when compared with its embrace of the world. It stands as a lone witness to God, towering over the wrecks of time.

Lost sheep find 'My Shepherd'; lost opportunity – 'I shall not want'; Lost soul – 'He restores my soul'; Lost righteousness – 'Paths of righteousness'; Lost loved ones – 'Valley of the shadow of death'; Lost anointing – 'You anoint my head with oil'; Lost blessing – 'My cup runs over': Lost mercy – 'Surely goodness and mercy shall follow me'; Lost life – 'All the days of my life'; Lost home or abiding place – 'I shall dwell in the House of the Lord for ever.' These are some of the lost sheep which are found in this anthem of assurance. We can echo the words that the

Prodigal son brought from the lips of his father and the woman who found the lost coin: 'Rejoice with me, for that which was lost is found' (Luke 15:9 and 24).

What makes this canticle so popular is the fact that every path of life converges into it, as lanes running into some main road. YOUR life travels right through this psalm. The Pilgrim Journey is here, the path YOU have trodden. Your weakness, your strength, your peace, your anointing, your table, your feelings – painful, poignant and pleasurable – are all set down here but, best of all, God and Jesus Christ are here! That which you are passing through at this moment, those two impostors, happiness and pain, are both here and they are dealt with by the Shepherd and Bishop of our souls. There are no tracts of land that His feet have not marked.

There is protection for the weak; healing waters flow into sickness; a quiet spirit and mind find their calmness here. It is at once a paradise and a sanatorium. There is friendship for the lonely, a sure path for the straying, life in abundance for the dying. Water flows into thirst and releases it. Goodness and mercy shall follow me every day, every hour, every year. The canzonet never ends. It has to be continued in your life. Let the rivers of quietness flow! Let the tender grass grow! Let the cup be filled to overflowing! There is a house in the place of the wilderness. Life is, and can be, more than swirling sands and changing scenes where all is swept away. The sheep are brought to a final resting place – the HOUSE OF THE LORD and the influence of God. That is what it can mean for you. In this descant you cannot find one shepherdless sheep. Not one is without leadership. There is no sheep without green pastures and gentle waters, for all are fed, all are led, all are brought into what is said.

Another thing which makes this psalm unique is that all the Names of God are suggested, almost as if you are gazing at water, and forms and shapes appear in the moonlight.

Jehovah-reah . . . 'The Lord is my Shepherd'; Jehovah-jireh . . . 'I shall not want'; Jehovah-ropi . . . 'He restores my soul'; Jehovah-tsidkenu . . . 'He leadeth me in the paths of righteousness'; Jehovah-shammah . . . 'Thou art with me'; Jehovah-sabaoth . . .

'In the presence of my enemies, the Lord of hosts'; Jehovah-nissi – The Lord my banner ... 'Surely goodness and mercy shall follow me'; Jehovah-gemulah – the Lord of recompense ... 'My cup runneth over – I shall dwell in the House of the Lord for ever'.

The truth, the whole truth and nothing but the truth about God. His way, His words, His works, His whole character is seen in every blade of grass and every quiet stream. It is almost as if David is looking at God through a kaleidoscope. The nature of the Shepherd which runs through every valley and flows from an overflowing cup. You do not need a crystal ball or to consult the stars when you have this dictum spread before you. It takes care of our past, our present and of our prospective. Hebrews 13:8, ' ... The SAME yesterday, today, tomorrow'. Let us come to it as sheep and graze. Let us come as those who would contemplate and gaze. Arrive as a beggar and leave as a Prince! Come in as a prodigal and go out as a son in sheep's clothing! Enter in at the narrow gate of the Lord ... leave by the vast open space of FOR EVER! Let us travel through the psalm as followers of Jesus and transformations will take place. The miracle power of God can operate in my life until I become a psalm, read of all men. Imbibe it until there is that transformation and the cup, overflowing, is mine. I want to be tender grass and waters of quietness.

The psalm opens with the word LORD. It closes with the word LORD. Only Lordship places God at my side as a Shepherd. See and hear, taste and know the devotion of that Shepherd to the sheep.

Let us take a deeper look at some of these things. 'He leadeth me ... He maketh me ... He anoints me ... He restores me ... He comforts me ... He follows me ... He dwells with me for ever'.

Then your devotion must be to the Shepherd. I must surrender and be led. I must be willing to follow. Jesus said, 'My sheep hear My voice and they follow Me' (John 10:4).

Do not stop at the first verse of the psalm, but go right through it until its music and healing are in your very soul. There are pastures, streams, valleys and cups, anointings, rod and staff, comfort; all are awaiting those who will follow.

One

The Lord Is My Shepherd

The Lordship of His Love

Great kings and mighty men have always seen themselves as shepherds who went before the people sometimes guiding, sometimes goading them onwards towards their goal. Very few led by example. Men of all nations and of all climates had their frailties and, as they died, the crowns fell from their heads and the vision disappeared from their eyes. The words which had fallen from their lips became lost in the dust of time.

We as Christians have a Shepherd Who lives in the power of an endless life (Hebrews 7:16). This means that He is able to see the plans right through to the end for every life! Our Shepherd can pick up the broken pieces, He can take the broken reed and make music from its shattering experience (Matthew 12:20). Jesus can take the knots of life and turn them into mountains of conquest. He shepherds for ever. Jehovah – ever living, ever present, ever in existence . . . always acting in the NOW because He is in the KNOW. God is a very present help in trouble. He is more present than the trouble! The God of the universe is among the flock. 'Behold the Lamb of God!'. He is one of us and so near to us who are so dear to Himself.

The language of the Hebrew is brought out in the Amplified Old Testament: 'The Lord is my Shepherd to feed, to lead, to guide and shield.' With God at the head you are always with the Leader.

Psalm 23 commences with the Lordship of God. It is only when Jesus becomes Lord at the beginning that we can know His Lordship in every part of believing, doing and caring and, as we move on, through reigning. Sheep are ruled and not ruined by touch, smell, hearing and responding. Lordship results in workmanship. God becomes a Shepherd, while men become sheep.

When the Lord is the Shepherd the sheep are well cared for. The green pastures, quiet waters and an overflowing cup are ours, standing on a full table. Such Lordship makes us and brings us near enough for God to fill and pour into as a cup until we overflow. No sheep is left out. They are numbered among the ninety and nine of Matthew 18:12 and are not left to die in the valley of tears, or to drown in an overflowing cup. The waters of quietness are only for a time. They are not allowed to stay there until the sheep pass through petrification and into stone statues.

Whatever the Shepherd does for the sheep He does it right where they are. Not in another pasture, some other valley or by quite a different stream, but right where we are within the Crown of His Lordship. He sends no messengers of some distant power. The grass is greenest where we are. The cup will be filled at the table where we sit. The rod and the staff will operate in the valley which you are in. He performs, as a Shepherd, miracles of grace – right where we are.

Christ Jesus is the GREAT SHEPHERD (Hebrews 13:20). He is the CHIEF SHEPHERD (1 Peter 5:4). He is the GOOD or BEAUTIFUL SHEPHERD, words that are used to describe good tasting wine without water, or corn without chaff (John 10:1). He is the SUFFERING SHEPHERD (Matthew 26:31), the BISHOP SHEPHERD (1 Peter 2:25). What He is must be born in us through a birth of the Spirit of God (John 3:6–8). Sheep and Shepherd have such a relationship as vine and the branch, or finger and thumb.

When a small boy was dying and needed the assurance of belonging to the Shepherd someone told him to count on his fingers the opening words of Psalm 23. The thumb, 'The'; first finger, 'Lord'; second finger, 'is'; third finger, 'my'; fourth finger, 'Shepherd'; and so on. They discovered the little one had died grasping his third finger . . . 'My'. There is the personal contact and the individual relationship. He loves every sheep as if all the flock were just one sheep. We can all claim Him as our own.

I personally can know His nearness, hear His voice, know His
walk and His talk. Shadows can become substance and thoughts
can become deeds. 'For me to live is Christ' (Philippians 1:21).
Paul slept, thought, spoke, lived Jesus Christ.

'MY' – whatever He is and has shall be mine. The cattle on a
thousand hills to the kettles on a thousand stoves need converting into 'MY' . . . My walk, talk, life and love, my all in all, until
I proclaim: 'My Lord and my God!' (John 20:27,28).

Every sheep is either a good or a bad testimony to the
shepherd. We use the word 'my' for very personal things. God,
in the Shepherd mould, is exclusively, essentially and eternally
MINE.

A call and a claim on the Shepherd brings such calmness into
troubled situations if it be 'you' bid me come to you on the
water, (Matthew 14:28).

The word SHEPHERD is a corner stone, and we build everything on that key stone. Luther remarked, 'Other titles for God,
such as Creator, Redeemer, Sustainer, Upholder are glorious titles
but they make God somewhat removed from us'. A God in the
clouds and up in the stars, even one in the trees, is no good for
sheep. They require a presence in the pasture. The staff of life
must be among the stuff of life. God is right here in this psalm.

'Jesus laid down His life' (John 10:11). To be a shepherd He
constantly lays down His life before us, as an example and as
an ensample. He has rights to certain things. The birth of Jesus
Christ came first to shepherds (Luke 2:8,9). The name of shepherd
brings Heaven to earth and God in Christ into the human span
of things. The word Shepherd in the Old Testament was the
parallel to the word Father in the New Testament.

David, through everyday happenings, does not see God in this
psalm as a shield or sun, a bow which he breaks asunder, a
sword or a spear. He sees Him as a living Friend. A friend is
one who steps in when the world steps out. He is with you as a
Shepherd in the dim light and in the dark. When the difficult
has to be dealt with, God is right there. David sees and knows
God as One Who is with the sheep. In the New Testament the
people could not tell Jesus from amongst the other disciples –
(John 18:4,5; 20:14). This Shepherd of ours walks and sleeps,

rises and wakes with the sheep. The pasture is the heart of the Shepherd. This is why Jesus became a man. When Jesus was born the Shepherd truly became one of the sheep. Jesus said, 'I am among you as One that serves'.

When David uses the words 'The Lord is my Shepherd', he places himself at the feet of, in the hands of, on the shoulders of, in the face of, and in the control of the Shepherd. Not to be butchered, but to be blessed. Not to be killed, but to be kissed (Luke 15:20). Remember that David had been a shepherd himself.

It is not amazing that the ancients called Psalm 23 'the Bible of the heart'. Paths of righteousness run through it as main arteries, with love flowing through the veins. The throb of God is here.

In our Shepherd we have displays of the absolute Divine and we catch glimpses of these attributes as we follow Him. 'No man spake like this man' (John 7:46). 'Come, hear a man who told me all things I ever did' (John 4:29). 'Jesus took her by the hand' (Matthew 9:25). At the wedding in Cana of Galilee He 'showed forth His glory' (John 2:11). When the water is turned into wine then we understand more of His Shepherd nature and Shepherd heart. Throughout the life of Jesus you will catch glimpses of the Shepherd's heart. The tender call of His voice will be heard, the staff will be fixed and the rod will be felt.

In the word SHEPHERD there is a thought of caring, sharing, leading, guiding, which is done in such a way as to make us follow in the footsteps of real love. Sometimes the sheep went along a narrow defile and, occasionally, through situations where they had to trust in order to triumph. They had to be goaded on occasions. Steep hills and sliding paths have to be met with the assurance of the Shepherd's ability for every situation.

The Gospels in the New Testament reveal a Shepherd for every situation of life. As we walk in love the tread is easy and the step is light. This Shepherd never leads us into the sling in order for us to be thrown out. He never leads or leaves us in the grasp of the bear or under the paw of the lion. He measures the gaps, the holes and the width of streams with his staff, making sure that the sheep are safe. We do not degenerate as we follow the Master into a lion or a wolf's den or mouth.

The largeness of your love for the Shepherd will determine the power and the ability of the Shepherd in your life. Ours can be a large flock, a large fold, tended by a large-hearted Shepherd.

Verse 1 of the psalm is not the Shepherd speaking; it is the language of the love of the sheep, not a bleating sound of discontent but one of sweet satisfaction from surrender. It is the lamb with its skip and its wagging tail. It is an expression of life in Christ. His ability to keep and shepherd is in the mind and on the tongue of the sheep. This is not tongue in cheek, but truth in Christ.

The sheep is making a declaration and a denunciation. 'The Lord is, the Lord *is* my shepherd. I will neither follow nor fear evil'. When 'ill' is compounded with any other word such as Ev-ill, it expresses badness of quality or condition. We follow not the like of evil, we follow the rare Shepherd.

There are paths and holes with thorns and fears which we are allowed to enter in order that we might learn to lean. His shoulders, not my ability, bear me along. The best time to approach a straying sheep is when it is at its weakest, and when we are melted by our own doings it is then that we embrace God's teachings through His reachings, and not through our reasonings.

Sometimes a shepherd will leave a sheep where it is. If it is placed on the edge of a cliff it might jump over if it is approached by the shepherd. If it is in a thicket it could struggle and do itself more harm, so the shepherd leaves it until it weakens. When one is drowning one has to realise that surrender to the person doing the saving is necessary for survival. Through the rocks, over the hills and spreading in the vales the call of His voice comes. As a blind person can hear a language in the tapping of his white stick which tells him of a wall, a hole or some other danger, so the sheep determine by the tapping of the rod the wisdom and knowledge of the shepherd. They know shapes and sights by the sounds of the tapping. They live in the echoes of that rod knocking against the stones, and peace is interpreted to them. It is in the difficulties that the sheep get to know the dynamism of their Shepherd.

The Shepherd always dwelt with the sheep. Their place was

his place. The cold sheep leant on him for warmth and his body sheltered them from the stormy blasts. The nearest to him were fed with small shoots and received encouragement. When the sheep was sick it leaned on the Shepherd. The weak sheep just leaned. When it was in need it adopted the leaning position as John the beloved Disciple did (John 21:20). All evil thoughts and fearsome things disappeared under the smile of the Shepherd. When the sheep was weak it was carried along and brought to the warm fire and to the milk. It is through the Shepherd's love that we are born, drawn, kept and fed.

Sheep are very shortsighted. That is why they need to keep close to the One who sees afar (Luke 15:20). When the prodigal son was a great way off, the father saw him. The Shepherd becomes the eyes of the sheep, seeing, interpreting, revealing what they can never know.

When we get into difficulties that is the time to cry, 'The Lord is my Shepherd'. That cry has toppled many a Goliath! It has run through many a troop! It will brighten our darkness and it will chase the wolf away. If Jesus is the Door, the wolf will not come to the Door. This phrase is our password and our distress signal. It resists temptation and evil, it makes weak sheep stronger than sin.

Every Shepherd was a war hero. They were armed lightly but fully to meet every emergency. They were fully equipped, and what manner of implements came from that little bag which the shepherd wore around his waist and near to his heart! What blessings and help are in the Atonement of Jesus Christ!

The sheep could only shake its wool at the enemy, they could only bleat, show their teeth, or even wag their tails! One word, one shout of command ringing through the valley, a stone from a sling, could dislodge rocks in the ravines, bring about an avalanche and bury the enemy. When the rod was applied with vigour the roar of the lion soon became the run of the lion! Roar became a rumour! The lion put its tail between its legs when it felt the rod between its eyes or ears.

Always remember that the sheep were the riches of the Shepherd. They were his investment, his white opals, his silver, his white gold.

John 10, particularly in the Revised Standard version, places great emphasis on the word 'OWN'. 'I know my own. My own know Me'. God doesn't keep sheep in the way a beekeeper keeps bees, knowing the hive but not the bees. God is not as a jailer who has all the keys to the locks and the cells but doesn't know the individual prisoners other than as a charge sheet. God KNOWS me as I am KNOWN. He knows every sheep as if there were only one. He said of Abraham: 'I KNOW him' (Genesis 18:19 – King James version). It is not the knowledge of looking at a sheep from the outside, but a knowledge of BEING on the inside looking out. It is a statement of character bred from closeness and from inspection. We all know the Monarch of the day. The Royal Family knows the Monarch; the husband knows the Monarch. God's knowledge of us and the Shepherd's knowledge of the sheep includes all three aspects of knowing. There is the knowledge of building, of making, of creating and of conversing. God knows and sees from every aspect. he doesn't even need telling, He KNOWS.

When asked how a shepherd knows sheep the reply was . . . by their defects . . . one lost ear, one lame leg, one slightly deaf, one with a limp, one partially blind. Some are known by their waywardness and their wanderings. Some are marked out by rebellion. Love covers a multitude of sheep, just as wool does in the natural. God perceives the depths, the darkness, the ditches and the despair we have entered into. It is the skill of the Shepherd, fully armed, which brings us safely into another day.

The trust of the sheep for the Shepherd is built up during times of crises and storm. They learn to trust even as humans do. Nature knows how many lemons to hang on a branch without breaking it! It is wise wisdom which only gives us four fingers and a thumb. We cling to enough and carry so much in our hands with what we have been given. Many times it can be too much for us.

The Lord knows us by the battles He has brought us through, and by the parts of our lives which have been touched by His grace.

Two

I Shall Not Be In Want

The Barrel and The Cruse which Fail Not

It is a great pity that we lift texts out of their context. This promise has nothing to do with prosperity, but its fulfilments are found in valleys of death, in sweet gentle streams and tender grass with overflowing cup. The promise is relevant to that which we undergo as we follow the Shepherd of our souls, as sheep.

'My God shall supply all your need according to His riches in glory by Christ Jesus' (Philippians 4:19). The supply is to bring that to us which needs furnishing, as if the heart were some empty house and God as a Shepherd begins to fill it with all manner of modern designs.

It is out of Christ's fulness that God fills our emptiness until we find that there is no lack to those who turn not back. Each sheep has on it the owner's brand mark. Every soul which belongs to God has stamped upon it by grace and with the hand of Divine authority the words of Ephesians 1:13 . . . 'I shall not be in want'. That state of being lost on the hillsides shall not be mine. That life without a Shepherd who has gone before will not be mine. I shall neither sit, stand or walk in want.

The wandering sheep will always be in want. Rebellion breeds want as hot sunshine results in a desert or breeds ticks in the wool of the sheep. In Luke 15:14, the Prodigal began to be in want. We tend to wander behind and be the tail rather than the head. We become inferior to what God the Great Shepherd has planned for us. We come short of God's best for our blessing. The end result can be starvation. Where the word 'want' is used in Luke 15:14, the same Greek word is used in Hebrews 4:1, describing coming short of the rest which God has provided for us. The scope of this promise is so large it includes every hair of my head and breath of my mouth. In the joy of the Lord your face will not lack a smile and your lips will not lack a laugh. The words of Jesus to Peter (John 21:15–17) . . . 'feed my lambs, feed my sheep. Shepherd my sheep'. Shepherded sheep are happy sheep, content with their lot. The words 'Feed my sheep' mean SHEPHERDISE. It suggests more than just gazing on them, tending to them, feeding, leading, guiding; it means an overflowing of the goodness of God, even as all the natural shepherd's powers operate for the good of the sheep. Whatever is best for the sheep is in the Shepherd's heart. Everything he does is an overflow of that heart. The blades of grass wave in the wind as those who are clapping and cheering the sheep along the way. He makes sure that we are safe. It is part of His nature to find us the best pasture. The sheep are the light of His eye both day and night. God, the source of sustaining power, who upholds the worlds by a word, is a God who will never walk lame, who will never grow weary or weak, who is at your side as a Shepherd to shepherd you through every deep gorge and over every high mountain. When your tongue bleats or your tail wags, God is there. He is a God who neither slumbers nor sleeps. So many times we have been like the dog chasing its own tail and thinking that, if we caught it, it would bring happiness. When I walk forwards I don't chase my tail . . . my tail chases me! The Shepherd follows the sheep and we have no need to chase Him.

The word WANT can describe a lack of wisdom, a lack of mercy, the lack of water for Noah's Ark when the waters abated (Genesis 8:3). That which Noah was to the sheep in the ark, God can be to you in your salvation. As water was to the boat or ark, so God is to the sheep as Shepherd.

WANT also can suggest a lack of righteousness, a lack of peace. No lack shall turn me back, it will only turn me to the hand of the Shepherd. 1. Kings 17:7 describes the lack of water. It suggests the brook which was dried up. All things are yours. In all these things God is saying through David, 'you shall not be in want if you follow the Shepherd. These things shall be pressed down, shaken together and running over'.

When we were pioneering a Church in Gainsborough, Lincoln-shire, every Monday morning for a number of weeks we would hear a knock on the door. When we went to open the door, that door became the hand of God to us, for one morning there would be meat, another morning fish, sometimes eggs, and so on. It was as if we had to write the shopping list and God had to fill the basket. The ravens which fed Elijah also came to that part of the world week after week and deposited their precious cargo right on our doorstep as we, without money or income, were praying. On another occasion I required a bookcase for my books. Not having finance to purchase such, I went to prayer knowing that God had said, 'I shall not want'. As I prayed I heard a bang outside and a voice spoke into my spirit . . . 'there is the bookcase you require'. I went to the window, expecting to see a furniture van from a large store delivering something to our address. All I saw was a pile of wood which had just been dropped, unceremoniously, by a workman in such a way as to send a shattering sound throughout the street! I looked at that pile of nailed wood and again the inner voice said, 'Get to work on that wood!' I did. I sawed, planed, nailed it, and made it into a bookcase. Nothing fashionable, but durable and reliable. God had answered my prayer and shown me that He supplies the answers in many different ways. Once again He had proved we would not be in want.

I once went through a phase when I was too embarrassed to give to people. Every time I gave, without fail someone would come and bring me double, and each time they would have a strange look on their faces as if they had been sent from Heaven and had been watching everything I had done! There is a whole environment in this thought of want. Where God is there is the whole of His creation for my delectation.

It is the voice of the Shepherd of the sheep which has helped over many a hill and brought through many a valley. It is the songs He plays to us as we travel which brighten the spartan rocks as we pass by. Many times the sheep has been rescued from want, be that want as crushing as a lion's paw or as wide open as the mouth of the wolf. The sheep have been lifted, carried, bathed and anointed many times, even resting where its bleat is lost in the heartbeat of the Shepherd. The sheep has every confidence in the Shepherd. It is satisfied with its lot in life. So many needs have been met through its life's journey – as many as the curls and whirls of wool on its back.

As the sheep travels it is as if the whole landscape is full of music from the Shepherd's reed. Every sunbeam shines, 'I shall not be in want'. Every brook gurgles the same thought. The valleys echo with this same confident shout. Even the birds of the air seem to whistle it in song and in sunshine.

This confidence was born out of experience and experiment which led to every enrichment for the sheep. Whenever it was dark God was and is there as Light. The Light of the World has no need to call for a light as the Philippian jailer did. He has no need to switch on and off. He is Light for ever. In troubled waters God was there as calm. The sheep have no hands, but God has. In deep straits God in Shepherd's clothing was there to straighten out. All the time God was placing things into the psalmist's heart and he was harping them out. David could look back upon his life and recognise the workings of the Shepherd on his behalf. He never went too high or sank too low for God to reach him or lift him.

When of mature years we tend towards this psalm as roots to water; it meets the needs of the sages of all ages. There is an old English proverb: 'The lion has need of the mouse'. The Shepherd has need of the sheep. They are His love baskets. They are the centre of His love, wrapped in balls of wool. God has never said that goats shall not want, only sheep. Those with all the markings of sheep shall not want. As they become like sheep, God becomes like a shepherd. A mother's motto reads like this: 'Cast your bread upon the waters and in many days it shall return unto you buttered'. When the sheep give their life to the Shepherd, the Shepherd gives His life to the sheep. Not all at once, but day by day and hour by hour. They need something different in the morning and they require something different at night. They require one thing when they are afraid and quite another thing when they are lambing.

Notice throughout this psalm how the personal touch is prevalent. 'He leads me . . . makes me . . . my soul . . . I walk . . . I will fear no evil'. When God is all good, why fear evil? Where good is present, evil is made to be absent.

Young lions, for all their prowess and natures, suffer and know hunger. That gentle, simple, tender sheep does not, because it does not rely on its own strength or what is within it as a reserve. It leans and learns to lean upon the Shepherd.

The Chaldee translates this phrase: 'They lack nothing'. Probably because they are nothing. Their highest and strongest point is the shadow of the shepherd with rod and staff. I cannot be in want – either now or in the future. The past has been dealt with. The winds of time have been allowed to blow upon the footmarks of the straying sheep and the dust covers their wanderings and all the evidence. Jesus died to release us from the pollution of sin, the power of sin, the penalty and the poverty of sin, and one day we shall be removed from its very presence. The Shepherd has scattered the dying embers of past flames and fires. He has arisen!

The shepherd was the door into the fold and the door out of it. No one came in or went out without his knowledge and permission. That applies to your past. While the Shepherd is counting the sheep He is naming them according to their characteristics. They are named by their natures. We are named with a new name, given to us through our new nature in Jesus Christ. He is also working out their needs so they shall not be in want. You have to see the many answers to prayer which David received between slaying Goliath and ascending the Throne to understand this. How can sheep want, when their Shepherd is the Creator of all the lands? His rod and staff are as straight and as strong as when the angels first sang their songs at Creation.

The story is told of a preacher who had no money to get to his next appointment. On his way he picked up an old stick or two and kicked a few loose stones around. As he walked, he saw something glittering on the end of a stick. It was a gold ring with the words 'God speed thee, friend' written on it.

Just as the great mountain will support every boulder, blade of grass and tree, so the Great Pastor will support His sheep.

Another translation of 'I shall not be in want' is 'He satisfies my every want'. The word used for WANT is the same as that used in 1 Kings 17:14 '... Neither shall the cruse of oil *fail*.' I shall lack nothing. The care of my Herdsman will never fail, even as that cruse of oil never failed. He cannot fail, for He is God. If He should fail every blade of grass should wither and die, and flash into a million fragments before the reaching tongue of the sheep touched it. If God should fail then every river would cease to flow and every cloud would be as dry as dust. The stars would cease to shine, and the moon would be green cheese indeed!

There are some lovely green pastures into which we are led out of the valley of death. All the paths of God do not come to a sudden end, they stretch into something deeper and wider for us. God is always at hand, on hand, by the hand ... Philippians 4:5. That is why, when the little boy fell from the window to seemingly certain death he was heard to cry, 'Alright Lord, Now is Your chance'. He escaped with just a few bruises!

The Lord is My Shepherd, that is all I want. He is all I need, all I require – all, because He is the All in All and has become my All in All.

A minister telephoned an advertisement to a newspaper in order for his Sunday Sermon to be printed. He said to the reporter: 'The Lord is My Shepherd'. The newspaper contacted the minister again. 'The wording you have given us is a little vague', they said. 'That is all I want', said the preacher. When the advert appeared in the newspaper it read ... 'The Lord is My Shepherd, that is all I want'.

He is all I need and He is all I require. The Love of God stretches from shore to shore, from north, south, east and west. It means that wherever I stand I stand in the centre of His love. He is the All in All, and He becomes my All in All.

In Matthew 17:24–27, when Peter was asked if his Master paid the tribute money, he replied, 'Yes'. Jesus told Peter to take a hook and receive a fish with money in its mouth to meet the need. Verse 27 says, ' ... Give it them for Me and for thee, Peter'. That miracle, that course of action was enough for both.

The death, the resurrection, the ascension and the Second

Coming of Jesus Christ is enough for all. What Jesus accomplished on the Cross as the Good Shepherd was enough to discover and dismantle all my wants. All my lack was placed on His back. All my straying was met by His staying on that Cross. When He cried 'IT IS FINISHED', He had you and me in mind!

Three

He Makes Me To Lie Down in Green Pastures

The Pleasantness of God's Pastoral Provision

That which God leads us into is neither barren nor unfruitful. He brings us to that which is green. There is plenty of it, but sadly it is by various means that God seeks to bend our paths into the finest pastureland for the sheep. That which we have chosen by our sheepish thinking, is leading to the barren, the bare and the bygone, leads us into fullest green.

Sometimes the shepherd has gone before, particularly if there is more than one shepherd, looking for the best pasture for the sheep at the time of their need. Jesus said: 'I go before you into Galilee'. Jesus was before you before you were born, and He will be before you when you die.

It wouldn't be unusual for the shepherd to bring a few tufts, a number of sprigs or shoots for the sheep to taste before they ventured into the pastureland. The sheep must not always be driven, they must sometimes be led. These words are a direct fulfilment of the previous promise – 'I shall not want' – met with the pastures of tender grass.

The sheep are not in the pen or the fold but are brought to a place where they might have life 'in all its fulness' (John 10:10, NEB). It is here that the lambs frisk, skip and jump, going through their tail-wagging ceremonies. These pastures are as important for sheep as any ship sighting land after a long voyage.

It is their eureka! We have found it! It was as important to the
sheep as a bee discovering the source of nectar.

There is a freshness and a sweetness about the word 'green'
which is sliced into pastures for the sheep. It is the first mention
of a colour in the sacred song.

The verb 'makes' is very strong in the original. God so leads
us into grace and glory that, like Peter and John, we feel it is
good for us to be here. It is God bringing us, by a variety of
methods, to the place where we will lie down. God wants us to
graze on His grace, He wants us to graze on His goodness. He
wants us to graze until the cup floods, running over with His
goodness and His mercy.

He 'makes' me to lie down in green pastures. The Hebrew
language is future, but it includes the present. What a difficult
task the shepherd has with the sheep who want to wander and
be on the mountains at night instead of being in the shadow of
the shepherd. The sheep want to be running, going, striving,
exploring, seeking, yet it is *resting* which the shepherd has in
mind. The leader of the flock must lead. We must get up from
the strawy bed and dried leaves. Straw and hay are symbols
of the old nature and life (1 Corinthians 3:12). The sheep had to
get up and get into something which would seem like Heaven
to them after they had been travelling a dusty old road. It was
and is the custom of the shepherd to lead the flock at high noon
to a place of rest from the noonday sun. God can cause our
restless strivings to cease. God can calm all the fears of our
feebleness . . . all the dustbowls of disillusion can disappear as
we trust Him. The sheep are being led into something which is
large enough for every sheep to lie down in. Tired feet, wracked
brain, dusty eyes, limbs which are limp with weariness, and a
tongue which is as dry as a piece of parchment through bleating
can all find rest.

If Jesus could and did calm a storm and sleep through it, stop
a funeral and release a maniac, then He can bring you to a place
of strength. There are many blades which have no cutting edge
in the pasture which God chooses for you. Apart from all that
which He carries, He can carry you. The shepherd who led them

in also led them through, and he led them out, taking them up and along the road to meet the next challenge.

His work is to get all the sheep to a position of being seated or lying down (Ephesians 2:6). This is the Epistle which tells us at its commencement that we are 'seated' and concludes with us 'standing' – (Ephesians 6:13, 14). Sitting, walking, standing are all in that book of Ephesians. The word 'sit' is to 'sit down with'. Where He is, I shall be, for ever.

God wants to bring us to the place where we pause for thought. A place where we think, where we rest in His reasons, where we place ourselves in His plans. Let all your pains be turned into peace as you rest. The position where we rest in grace and do not resist Him. God is your green keeper. He that keeps you and all there is to be kept will neither slumber nor sleep.

He 'makes me, He leads me, He restores me, He comforts me'. When we are in the right position in green pastures, God can work on us as we become the model. He does it with gentle breezes and with tender blades. God can then pour into us what the world has taken out of us. He lashes us with gentle sunbeams. What the sheep has lost in travel, it can gain in triumph as it is made to lie down. Jesus set the example for us in everything. He laid down His life (John 10:15–18) and because He laid down His life, then He could lay down sheep in tender grass. It is God's gentleness which makes us great. It turns lambs into sheep and mutton into lamb! It is the laying down process which allows sheep to stretch to their full capacity.

On occasion the sheep turn and gaze at the shepherd. John the Baptist was correct when he said, 'Behold the Lamb of God Who takes away the sin of the world'. If you want to know where you are and what you are, then look at Jesus. 'Let us fix our eyes on Jesus, the author and perfecter of our faith . . .' – Hebrews 12:2 (NIV). Let us keep gazing on Him as we are grazing.

Sheep are not tied to a stoop with a short rope; they are anchored to the Shepherd as they keep taking a look at Him. They measure their peace by their constant looking at the Shepherd. Their welfare state is in Him. He 'makes' me to get everything around me to blend together for my good. Everything that happens is as blades of grass which work together for my good until I reflect on the goodness of God in the land of the living. God can lift my heart into His plans when I am made to lie down. He is fitting me for the next step, the next journey. Elijah had to be fitted to go from the brook Cherith on to Zarephath.

Another version of the Bible puts it this way: 'He lays me down'. Just like the shepherd would lay down a newly born lamb by the side of its mother. When life knocks you off your feet, stay there until God picks you up again! You might be legless and sightless – but God isn't heartless. His heart is the shape of green pastures for you.

Most theatres have a Green Room, where actors can go and rest themselves prior to a performance. Jangled nerves, jangled in the jungle of human existence and experience, can find rest. The jostle is turned into sweet harmony at His side. The result is harmony and radiancy. Tensions relax in the green room.

We are at our strongest, not when we are skipping, jumping or running but when we are sitting, like Mary, at the feet of Jesus (Luke 10:39). When we lie down we are at our strongest and God is doing His most perfect work. When we lie and lounge in love, when we rest in realism, then we rest in Redemption.

Sheep need a sleeping place, a watering place, a feeding place and a resting place.

There is an old tradition that, when anyone was irritated in Bethlehem, they went and took a look at Jesus Christ and all their troubles just melted away, like a sheep eating green fresh grass.

In these pastures of tender grass the songs from the shepherd's pipe were heard. That is why we have bandstands and brass bands in our municipal parks.

In discipline there is sure, tender grass for the hungry sheep. For the sheep to lie down is a discipline which it must accept if it is to be well fed. When Jesus performed the Miracle of the Feeding of the Five Thousand (Matthew 14:17–21; Mark 6:39,40) the passage states, 'There was much grass in that place', and when it says, 'They were seated in ranks', the word is *florets*, which were like little clumps of flowers, placed like flowers in a bouquet, sitting and lying like white lilies amongst the grass.

The word 'etiquette' is from the French and means 'a floret or a border of flowers where every one is placed in its correct order and position'. When God wants to arrange a life like a bunch of flowers He brings us and makes us to lie down in green pastures until all our lives are in an orderly fashion. When we need to find the etiquette of Eternal life and life in the Spirit God brings us into grace as sheep into green grass and causes us to surrender to that measure of grace He has for us (John 1:16): 'Grace for grace' (King James version); 'Blessing upon blessing' (NIV).

When amber beads are made they have to be rested for a while because the amount of electricity passing through them would shatter every molecule, hence the time of resting.

We all love fields of bluebells, buttercups, daisies, cowslips – but we also need the green grass. Life can never be all flowers; there have to be grassy portions. That is when nature, under the Hand of God, takes us into her school to learn the many lessons she can teach us. Green is the colour in Creation which God uses the most. It is a restful colour. That might be the reason why city offices use green blotting paper – when you are about to write a letter in anger the restful, resourceful green can make you think twice about the words you are using. It almost has a message of quietness for your spirit. It is also the reason to have village greens and parks in areas where there are such depressing tenements.

God, in His wisdom, has broken up the Christian pilgrimage with patches of tender grass. It is not all green grass, and it isn't all cups which overflow, but it is goodness and mercy, whatever happens to us as His sheep.

Paul writes to one Church, in Philippians 4:10 . . . 'Your care for me has "flourished" again'. It had sprouted again. Something had entered into another springtime, into another patch of tender grass. There is that in us and for us which God wants us to lie in which can grow again. Groans can be turned into growth, in God. Let God care for you. Let Him reveal that care. When you enter into it you can flourish again. May the grey be supplanted by the green.

Pasture is a comely place. It is that which is at the right time in God's time. The root word from which we obtain the word 'pasture' is rendered in another place . . . 'pleasant' . . . describing the love by which Jonathan was knitted to David (2 Samuel 1:26). It describes the land which Lot chose in Genesis, which was well watered. In the Song of Solomon 1:16, Solomon says, 'Our bed is green'. The greenness of first love is alluded to. When we come to green pastures we arrive at first love for Christ. The green is a type of nuptial love. It is love for the Lord of love.

One man carried out an experiment with colours. He asked various age groups to complete a small questionnaire. Red was the most popular colour with children. Blue was the colour which appealed to youth. However, when those of mature years were questioned, it was green which was unrivalled. 'He makes me to lie down in green pastures'. In mature years there is no need to come to a stop, there are lots of green pastures in God's field of fulness.

Sheep, by virtue of their very natures, find it difficult to lie down and relax. They are difficult to control when the shepherd tries to make them lie down. Watch them being dipped or sheared and you will see a battle of wills! Will it? Won't it? In that position they feel weak and at a disadvantage, yet many times it is all for the good of the sheep. It is in those positions that the shepherd can minister oil to their wounds, sealing up their sores, and food can be found close at hand.

Sheep will lie down if certain conditions are met:

(a) They must be free from lurking fears;
(b) There must be no friction amongst them;
(c) They must not be tormented by parasites or other foreign bodies;
(d) They must be free from hunger;
(e) They must be able to see the shepherd and sense his presence;
(f) The presence and power of evil must be removed;
(g) They must lie down, sheep with lambs, and with the shepherd.

The green grass is full of vitamins for the sheep. It is rich with the vital refreshment they need and it also contains healing properties. Each blade of grass is a bucket of provision. Not all blades are swords or knives, certain grasses assist with the healing of eye diseases and disorders. They put strength and skip back into the sheep. Theirs is the joy when in pastures green. These grasses build them up so they can resist disease. Once the shepherd has dealt with the foes outside – the lion, the bear, the wolf – he ministers to the needs within.

If your vision of Christ is dim then learn to lie down in the green pastures of God. 'Come unto Me all you who are heavy laden and I will give you rest'.

If sheep continually travel the same old way, doing the same thing day after day, they get bored and fractious. They create a dust which carries parasites. They will create holes by using the same pathway and into these holes they will stumble. The blind will lead the blind. They will fall and break legs, leaving scars as memories of the way.

God is very tender in His dealings with us. He wants to lead us into mercy, the mercies of green grass, rather than into judgement. He wants to lead us the way of the lamb, rather than the way of the bear or the briar. The sheep need to rest their legs, even as human hearts, minds and spirits need rest.

There are certain things you will rarely see in tender grass – a ringing bell or an alarm clock, or a boat being rowed. God has to bring us to these places. When a youngster was asked to sit down, he did so very reluctantly, stating quite firmly: 'but I am not sitting down inside!'.

What tender grass there is in our salvation! The Shepherd beside us, Heaven ahead of us, the overflowing cup waiting for us, the anointing oil flowing towards us, wayward wanderings left on the hillsides behind us.

In John Bunyan's 'Pilgrim's Progress', Pilgrim was led to a green land called the Land of Forgetfulness. Forgetting the hardness of the way and the Giant Despair we need to come to a place in our lives called 'Manasseh' – Forgetfulness. We need to forget our past and look to the future, never forgetting the love of God which brought us to such rich and fulfilling pastures.

Four

He Leads Me Beside Still and Quiet Waters

The Quiet Waters of Acquiescence

There are beautiful pictures of security in Psalm 23. What God provides, He provides in abundance. Mountains so high we cannot climb them; seas so deep we cannot fathom them; flowers, so many we cannot count them; and stars so multiplied that we cannot follow them. Here the sheep have pastures of green, a cup that is full and running over, goodness and mercy following all the days of life. Here it is quiet waters in abundance. They are guided to where the sheep are restful.

It is almost as if the soul is saying, 'Rest, take your ease, God is for you, God is your friend and not your enemy'. The thief, the wolf, may break through to kill, steal and destroy, but these waters trickle round our feet as emblems of clouds dispelled and distilled into something better for us. 'My God SHALL ... SUPPLY ... ALL ... your needs ... ACCORDING to His RICHES ... by Christ Jesus' (Philippians 4:19).

In these waters life-saving acts are unnecessary! They are measured to the mouth and they are near to the need. There are no waves here, no millions of people passing through, as at the Red Sea. Pharaoh's chariots have sunk from sight and receded from hearing. The Voice of Jesus has commanded tranquillity – 'Peace, be still'. Spiritually the sheep are walking on water. Liquid quietness is now being poured into their souls. They cannot bleat and drink at the same time. The howling wilderness, the harassment of the parasites and the dimness of sight have all ceased. Noises from without and fears from within, jeopardy from around them, from swooping eagle or falling rock, have been commanded to stay. God leads us from all these things into these waters of quietness in order that we may drink and drink again. As the coolness, clearness and crispness of peace fills the soul, the worries and the pain seem to drain from us. We feel that we have been led to streams of salvation and pools of peace in plenty. Each pool or stream becomes a preacher to the soul of sores. We are like the little boy who was taken to the seaside for the first time. When he saw the sea he ran from the bus straight into the waters. He thought it was going to disappear!

This is an idyllic picture of any believers who are controlled by their connections with Jesus Christ. There is a quietness, a tranquillity through trust in Him. It is the picture of the sheep lying down at the waterside in the shadow and in the presence of the shepherd. It is a strange fact that our word 'bedlam' is a corruption of the word 'Bethlehem'.

We are being led to the place where we say: 'Lord, it is good for us to be here'. The spur and the shout, the rod and the staff, the hustle and bustle have all been wrapped into the tranquil. The tranquil will bring us through any trial and into triumph. It is as it will be in Heaven, as a sea of glass where we are brought to rest (Revelation 15:2).

Peace is a joining together, not a getting away from. It is nearer, still nearer, so precious are you. The sheep are joined to the shepherd. He is not away over the other side of the water. He is standing, sitting, working on the same side the sheep are occupying.

The Apostle Paul says: 'May the peace of God rule your hearts'. May it be as some Umpire in the Empire of God – putting things right which are wrong and pointing out the plans of God for life (Colossians 3:15). The peace of God is like a Roman Garrison, stationed around the heart and life, at every weak point and at every entrance to control the disturbers of your peace and to threaten them with the Throne. This peace is not only stillness and quietness, it is forever-ness, with firmness and fathoms in depth.

It is not to Sinai, with its belching, flaming fire and shaking earth that we have come. The colour green and still waters are exponents of grace. The shout of victory and the clap of accomplishment may be in these waters, but when we come to them it is the recognition of God's care which brings peace.

Left to their own wanderings the sheep would fall under the paw of the bear or into the open mouth of some wolf; to the noisy cataract or the muddy pool they would come, as if keeping a long-standing engagement. We, left to ourselves, would come to that which would frighten us even more, and, being terrified, we would go for more terror. We have not come to the noise of the trumpets but to the Voice of Jesus. Let Him reign in the ranges and ragings of life; let Christ take the torment out of your hell. He knows how to break the monotony. The sheep came here, even as we might visit some picture gallery. Jesus said, 'Come ye apart awhile'. He did not say, 'get away from it all', but – 'Come ye apart with Me'. If the world is tearing you apart, then make Christ the King of your heart. The world may snatch things from our grasp but that emptiness which is left can be filled with the Good Shepherd.

We all, as sheep, need a change of climate and environment, a change of scenery, of diet, or companions, but not a change from Christ, for He changes not, and you are dear. It is we, with our sheepish natures, who need changing. God can do it in a moment, in the twinkling of an eye! The only change we need from Him is fresh footprints as we follow on to know the Lord. Where Christ is, the quietness and well-being of the Eternal nature is formed into waters of quietness. Here there is heard the message of the still, small voice.

He leads me. He has the reins in His hands. His call comes over the mountains and through the valleys, leading me on to that which I need at this time in a timeless salvation away from a tormenting situation.

It is not to the stale and the stagnant, nor to the brackish and the bitter, but to that which is flowing gently onwards. God wants to lead you beside still waters, waters of gentleness and comfort, so that you can hear His voice and see your reflection as you gaze into the liquid love. God's full stops and steps are sometimes pools of quietness.

He 'leads' me. The word 'lead' in Isaiah 3:12 means 'to declare happy'. In Psalm 23, there is blessing in it. It suggests being made straight and going forwards. Operations take place at the still waters. While we are there the missing piece of the jigsaw can be put into place. While we are there the wool is growing, the heart is being enlarged and the saints, the sheep, can be perfected. 'Perfecting' is the putting back into place of a dislocated joint; it is the strength being replaced into empty shells (Ephesians 4:12). Shells become sheep again. Husks find they are filled with a new fulness. That which is wrong with our spirits is rectified by His Spirit. Water is a type of the Holy Spirit – His silent workings through His graces which have the goal of God's glory. God leads Jacob – that struggling, supplanting, crafty side of us, that resisting element – like a flock to this area of help. It was the shepherd's ministry fulfilled when he brought the lambs to the water. Jesus said, 'If any man thirst let him come unto Me and drink'. He is the Fountain of Life. In Him we can be washed clean and be refreshed.

The shepherd sometimes created these waters with his own hand. If the waters were too noisy then, by damming a stream, he could direct the flow of water towards a place where he could guide the sheep. When Jesus died the waters of Noah's flood, which spoke of the wrath of God, were redirected in grace towards thirsty hearts and souls which were longing for God and for good. Jesus didn't build a dam . . . Jesus was the dam. He stopped that which would have swept us away and in so doing turned it into a peaceful pool.

There is no Meribah or waters of strife here. There is no Marah or waters of bitterness. There is no chiding, only consoling. He brings us to that which shows His care and reflects our image in the still waters. It is a reflection of the life of the believer in God. There must be a certain early dew about our discipleship. There must be times when we all go to the shallow still waters of quietness. We still need quiet times during which we can surrender to the silent hand of God or call of God. Refreshing times are revival times.

It was the shepherd's work fulfilled to bring the sheep to a place where they could be happy enough to increase, for that is what happened at the quiet waters. He provided these waters by building a dam and causing them to deepen in one place where the sheep could get to them. There are promises of God which, when they are put together, form a cup for us to drink deeply from. There are times in life when the Shepherd redirects streams to pour into us and help us in the time of our longing thirst.

When there was no water to dam, then the shepherd carried shoots and cuttings from trees to help the sheep obtain moisture. The sheep are dry and thirsty. It only rains twice each year and by the time the rains come to fill the pools the sheep are weary and every step is a jolt to the whole system. The ground is hard on which they walk. They have lost their sense for other things. Only the scent of water fills their nostrils. They long for water which is in the hands and the guidance of the shepherd. It may be just around the next rock or over the next hill or even to the water's edge, but even if they were too weak to get there the shepherd would carry them. He even carried a little water with him in his pouch and he would wet the lips of the driest of the sheep. If they keep faithfully following they will be led to fountains of love. The ready-made cup will be theirs to drink from.

When they came to quiet waters they did not have to cross them, see them parted or walk on them. We try to do what God never intends that we should do. In the Parable of the Sower and the Seed (Luke 8:6) the plant withered because it lacked moisture. 'Moisture' is the normal word for a human body which lacks fluid. It has become dehydrated. As seed and growth need moisture, we need resting and refreshing rivulets in what Jesus Christ is, and what He has provided for us. John saw in Heaven such quiet waters and they had been transformed into a sea of glass (Rev. 15:2). The waters are needed to fill the ruts and put new life into old sheep. Dry and dusty sheep need to be filled again with water ... the freshness of it, the sparkle of it, the shock of its coldness needs to enter their bodies, as the Holy Spirit needs to come into the believer. Sometimes the sheep's journey is measured between quiet waters. Every road, every lane is leading to the pool of plenty. The empty are being led to the full. Jesus can carry us to the waters as a shepherd carries his sheep. He can take us there as a jug to fill us with His calm repose.

Still waters: waters of rest, waters of quiet rest; rest so plentiful that it can be measured in litres, it can be brought in cups that are overflowing to the quivering lips of the sheep. When God puts a full stop at the end of a sentence it is as big as a pool, and very often it is found in quiet waters.

Waters of rest: rest-giving waters, waters of resting places where the sheep lie, as flowers or lilies around a pond of plenty. The waters are good if the shepherd's feet lead to the edge. Where his feet stop and stay, there will I lie. 'Your God shall be my God and your people my people'.

It is quite amazing how and in what circumstances these waters are found in the Christian life. God sees that they are situated at the right place, just before the valley, and just after the cutting rock has been dealt with. Into the dynamic, into the gloom and the doom, into the desperate need and the new dimensions, these waters flow, measured by the rod of God. The stone He rolled away from the tomb at the Resurrection He uses to dam the waters in order to create waters for us. They can flow for us because Christ the Rock has been smitten, and those smitten pieces of rock dam the waters. God can break open your circumstances. He can make them flow. It was so important that Israel conquered Jericho for it was a city of fountains.

A true translation is 'resting places'. Just as your foot needs floor and the bird needs place on the branch, so sheep need these waters of quietness. God's sheep need them as part of God's provision for them. We need times of sweet repose, even as John did when he rested on the bosom of Jesus (John 13:23). Jesus still says: 'Come ye apart and rest awhile'. Come into the boat. Come away from it all and be refreshed.

There is a saving element in these waters. Without them the sheep would be driven too much and they would lose their young. They are life-saving and health-keeping, as is everything God provides for us: God's patches of plenty in pools of water. These pools, or streams of stillness, have no need to be our silent tears. That which comes from the Heavens has been placed at the feet of the sheep by the Shepherd.

When an army needed new recruits they sometimes brought them to the running waters where they were sworn in (Judges 7:5–7). They made their pledge to be as swift as the flowing waters and to overflow the enemy.

We need quiet resting waters to break up the monotony and to break up the scenery, to give the sheep something else to gaze upon.

It also meant rest, not only for legs, but for eyes – 'That the eyes of your understanding might be opened'. They needed gentle sounds, not the harsh sounds of falling rocks and running feet. David longed for the waters of Bethlehem (2 Samuel 23:15) – the waters that reminded him of his youthful days of zeal. To be at those waters and to drink again is refreshing indeed. He was in the midst of battle, needing that which reminded him of his youth and zeal, so he sent out a message, not for any old water, not the stagnant waters of religion, but for water from the well of Bethlehem! A cup of those waters would put new life into him. A cup of water from the place where it all started for Jesus as a Man, in Bethlehem. It is cooling and enriching. He needed waters from the place of childhood, the place of boyhood, the place of manhood. The waters of first love for Christ – how sweet they are!

The sheeps' eyes may be quite dim now through lack of water. As they drink deeply then vision is restored, legs are strengthened, they are emboldened to go on. They go softly like the waters of Shiloh. As the sheep drink it is almost as water to the clay to re-form them again into skipping sheep. Sheep and believers who have lost their skip and their joy need to draw water from the wells of salvation. These are the waters of refreshment and they give off a coolness for overheated lambs, ewes and rams.

As they arrive at the waters they come face to face with their own reflection. It is the work of the Spirit to convict, to illuminate, to sanctify and to bring holiness into the lives of believers. Although they came as a flock they individually had to drink and peer into those clear waters. There was such a happening when any Israelite Priest came into the Tabernacle. The waters in the laver were there before they could approach God (Exodus 30:18).

These waters are so different from the waters of Damascus, Abana and Pharpar which are vile and foul compared with the waters which God brings us to. Those waters are fresh from the mountain slopes of Calvary.

You will never know yourself or adjust your living to be as holy as God requires by looking at rocks, or fearing wolves, treading through sand or looking to the skies. The answer for all is quiet waters to rest your soul in God. Sometimes as sheep we get out of pasture, as flying objects out of orbit. Lame and sick sheep stayed by those waters until they received their full healing under the ministry of the shepherd. There is coolness without coldness. Nothing ever freezes to death here. They were washed down. Infections are cleansed and fresh oil applied.

God does not lead us to anything and then shove us in. He always goes before, even as the shepherd would sometimes go into the water first to make sure the sheep would be alright. The cup you are called to drink from has the mark of the lips and the life of Jesus before you touch it. There is a calmness without deadness. The sheep are being led just as much by waters of quietness as they are along a path up the side of a mountain or through the valley of death. Lack of activity needn't mean absence of assurance.

As we graze we gaze at the edge of the water. God's love is now shaped into something else, pools of cool clear refreshing water. What God provides He provides in abundance. Still waters – plural. God treating sheep with his love in abundance, as if the Thames river was flowing to quench the thirst of a blackberry growing on its banks. So much given and so much left, just like it was in Matthew 15:37 – seven 'hampers' is the wording, according to Dr Robert Young.[1] There was even an abundance left over after the Miracle!

I don't suppose the sheep could or would drink all the water. They left some for others who would follow. Leave a blessing behind you! Leave a pool for someone else to drink at. Dig wells as Isaac did for others to possess.

Note again the plurality – waters – denoting abundance, freeness, continuity. They were not meant to live on a rain drop or a splash caused by a stone. Nor were they expected to live on a ripple. Water in abundance is God's order for all who are thirsty in their following after Him (Revelation 7:17). This, to the sheep, was a little bit of Heaven on earth. They shall not only follow, they shall flow on in waters of quietness.

Five

He Restores My Soul

The Rectifying Reach

There are those who think that the psalm should commence with these words, words which are placed here so that none may despair and that none may presume on the goodness of God.

There is the initial restoration when we come to Christ and then if any man sin there is an advocate with the Father. We are being changed (2 Corinthians 3:18) 'From glory to glory' (King James version) or 'with ever-increasing glory' (NIV version). If the sheep, or the saints, slide and lose their footing or miss the way, it is the Shepherd who seeks us and brings us back into the fold.

Sometimes the word which is used to describe the sin is not enough. We call it sin, a falling away, a departure, an iniquity, a transgression, but words alone do not tell the full story of sinning or of restoring. In the fall there may be a breakage, there can be that which is torn limb from limb. Sin may be in the soul just as thick as the wool that is on the back of the sheep. That need for restoring may be seen in a rut, in a crevice, in a hedge, a cave, a precipice, a ledge or a ditch, yet God restores us from all these positions to the side of the Shepherd. If any man be in Christ he is being made into a new creation. At the heart of that new creation there is restoration.

The crook reaches into every crisis. The rod goes into every realm with authority. The Cross still works wonders in the soul of the straying saint. The soul can never fall too far for God to rescue it. The goodness of God is greater, deeper and higher than our wanderings. We cannot wander beyond His care. If feet could walk off the earth then maybe we could wander where God is not. Wherever we are, we are part of His Creation. Any wandering sheep is a challenge to the faithfulness of God. God is everywhere and where I am is part of that everywhere. If God's love is everywhere it is here, now. Where I am is right at the centre of it.

That restoration leads to a ministry of reconciliation. God works from every part in order to grant me a new start. That faithfulness is channelled into the many highways and byways into which we venture. A soul may stumble and fall because it cannot accept what God has made it.

There is a story told of a woman who could not accept that she was one of God's sheep. No matter which Scripture was quoted or whatever she was told, the reply always came back that she thought she was a goat and had a goat's nature! The counsellor got a little exasperated and, at the end of a very long session, said to her: 'Now listen here, you old goat! God has made you a sheep and not simply a bleat!'

One day a man was doing some work at the Church and he had with him his dog. The dog suddenly headed for the vestry and sought to go in, maybe for counselling or to be turned into a sheep – or at the least a sheepdog!! If God says we are sheep, we are sheep, even if we are somewhat sheepish!

There are times when sheep, by nature and desire, will not only stray but will fall into a hole. On other occasions they will linger so long that a bear or a wolf will come to take them off into the woods. That which has known the companionship of the shepherd is left to defend itself and to escape if it can. If we walk not humbly, following the Shepherd, the teeth of the wolf or the claw of the bear can soon make us to be just tails of wool blowing in the breeze. There are shadows and movements which would drive a whole hillside between the sheep and the shepherd. Attacks which lead into a need for restoration can come from every angle, through the known and the unknown, through the seen and the unseen, appearing in the expected and the unexpected. Many a sin has made its home in the words 'I never expected that to happen!' I take comfort that the first four letters of restoration spell *rest*.

The Gospel of Jesus Christ may be condensed into this one text – 'He restores my soul'. It is the Lord's love, the Lord's life and the Lord's liftings which restore to the soul the strength it needs to go on.

Someone has described this text, 'He restores my soul', in these words: 'A King's Son born; a King crowned; a Kingdom established'.

The word used here for 'soul' is a word used elsewhere for life. All that which life is and can contain. When God restores a person He restores the whole person. Pictures and paintings are restored regularly so that the artist's brushmarks can be clearly defined. God restores us into life, into the life of God which is more than the life of the grass on which the sheep graze. The overflowing cup can run dry; the oil can be stayed; the still waters can evaporate. The restitutional ministry of the Shepherd goes on for ever. It is not the ministry of the day alone but of the night and through the night, even through the years. It is good to know that His years fail not. Our years may be folded up as a garment, worn away or thrown away, but it is not so with the character of God (Hebrews 1:11).

He restores the soul to nearness. He restores the soul to the Shepherd's touch. He restores the soul to the paths of the Shepherd's choosing. A restored soul is a redeemed and forgiven soul. The believers at Thessalonica turned from idols to serve the Living God. In Luke, Chapter 15, the son is restored to the father, the coin to the hand, the sheep to the shepherd.

The word 'Restore' in the English language is from the Latin 'restauro' – 'to stand'. It puts you back on your feet! The skittles of life may have been knocked over but there is a Shepherd Who puts our feet onto a path. It places you where the Shepherd can be seen, followed and obeyed. The grass is at its greenest and the waters are at their sweetest when the soul has been restored.

As G. Wade Robinson says in his glorious hymn:

'Heaven above is softer blue and earth beneath a sweeter green. Something lives in every hue, Christless eyes have never seen'.

There must be something to be lifted from and Someone to be restored to. The Shepherd's hands and weapons are far greater than any situation into which the sheep may wander. Whatever the situation, however strong the bear or cunning the wolf, in the Shepherd the sheep have One to match all situations. 'All power is given unto Me in Heaven and in earth' (Matthew 28:18). Jesus does not have to go and collect it or borrow it on your behalf. It is given already.

The word used by the sheep to describe the restoring power of the Shepherd is the Hebrew word, 'shub' meaning to 'add to'; to add to anything that which is lacking. Adding sugar to coffee or salt to food. That which will make anything operate again as it was intended to operate. Mankind away from God does not operate as God intended. Take a lock; it holds the door closed and keeps out the intruder, but without the key it cannot operate fully. Without the Shepherd the sheep is at a loss. Every path leads into a cul-de-sac. Every way reaches a precipice. Light dims into darkness. We need the calling, assuring, sharpening voice of the Shepherd to help us and keep us. There is a thought in restoring of turning back, bringing back, leading back. There are steps in God backwards – which are forwards. God found Paul knocked off his donkey and, no doubt, knocked off his feet. The first step and the ninety and ninth step are repentance, a turning from that which has turned us from God. Turning that off which has turned you off from God.

Those things you have lost can always be found in the presence of the Shepherd. They are to be found where they fell. Why or where they fell can tell the story of where they were found.

There are three parables in Luke, Chapter 15, in which Jesus illustrates loss: the lost coin, the lost sheep and the lost son. One rolled away, one walked away, one strayed away. The manner of our exodus is not important, but the matter of our entrance is.

There are times when the grass is greenest on the other side, but that depends on the direction of the sun and on cloud formation. Stolen waters often appear to taste better than those things which God provides. We can make our own holes in the hedge using excuses which just lead into the open mouth of the lion. It is amazing how curly bits of wool can soon become as horns! That boulder we just wander around turns out to be the large paw of the bear. That voice which was muffled by many others turned out to be nothing like the voice of the Shepherd or the tune played on his reed. It was the voice of the evening wolf. Jesus said: 'I am come that they might have life' (John 10:10). As the empty cup is filled, as the barren is turned into green grass, so God can transform the life as He fills it. Restoration always results in life anew. To feel and to know and to see the strength of the Shepherd exercised on your behalf is restoration indeed! The winter has passed, the cold lonely night has gone, the bare branch has something perched on it. 'The winter has ended, the summer has come and the singing of the birds is with us'. The dawn chorus is in the soul. It is the shepherd body, arms and legs which put new life into lost sheep as they are lifted. The more weak and feeble they are the nearer they are brought to the leader – then the safer they are when they're laid at his feet before the open fire.

The lively and sharp claws of the bear, the wolf, the lion and other marauders sever our relationship with God. One of the first things the wolf or the fox will go for is the tongue of the sheep, to stop it calling, bleating its dying cry. Satan would stop you praying, calling, crying for help. When we cry, God is all hearing. He is all searching, all seeking, arriving, lifting and loving towards those who repent. God adds the tears of Jesus to your tears. He is able to succour those who are tempted. He is able to place wrappings around us as 'helps' were placed around a ship in a storm. The blood of Christ speaks and it strikes the binding forces, and we are set free. When we are restored we come as Israel from Egypt. The exiles come from the barren deserts of sin into the banqueting house, where a large table is spread. The days of the mirage have ended – the Eternity of Miracles is with us.

It is not only a hoof or an ear with a piece of wool which our Leader restores. It is much deeper than that. It is deeper than the blades of grass, and deeper than flowing waters. It is the soul which is restored. God does something to our inner self when He restores us. The sheep is not just led or thrown back among the flock, it needs special care. Paul nourishes and cherishes the newly restored souls (I Thessalonians 2:7). The word 'cherish' means to treat as a nurse treats her children. The shepherd, as he brings heat and life to body and limb is seen blowing his breath into the mouth of the sheep, rubbing it and rocking it until warmth and life returns. Doing what Elisha did with the Shunammite's son (2 Kings 4:34).

Away from the Shepherd we are travelling paths which are not the paths of righteousness. They are rutted and rough with difficulties. They are paths which are crooked, and they lead to the crooked man, the crooked house, the crooked lane, the crooked speech, the crooked walk. Everything has a strange twist which smacks of the tail of the serpent. We can have lives which are as the house which Jack built, everything all over the place, without order. Everything crooked. Lives can be like pieces of broken bread rather than as the Bread of Life sent down from Heaven.

The way of the backslider is hard. The waters where we rest bring no rest at all, they are anything but quiet. They are agitated. 'Let not your heart be troubled' (John 14:1). Troubled like a stormy sea. In John 14:1 we have the troubled sea but also the ship's anchor – 'believe in Me'. The port is there: 'Believe in God and believe in Me'. The Captain is in the text: 'Trust in Me'. Faith calms the waters; it puts the swell into our hearts. We enter into valleys where we do fear evil. The cup which we hold is a religious cup filled with ceremony, and we are always drinking the dregs. Ours is the last wine – not the first. Ours is the last drink and not the first. There is no sweetness there. The green grass is full of weeds and poisonous herbs. In our wanderings we are only allowed to wander until we find the bitter hyssop of repentance which needs to be dipped into the blood, as Israel were commanded to do for their restoration (Exodus 12:22). In our wanderings we never wander beyond His fold, for that is the world at large. God can bend our ways into His way. So often we are like the donkey in Mark 11:4 – there is a door for us to enter but we are tied, limited, and unable to enter that door. It takes a message from the Chief Shepherd to release us and use us. We need to be reached out for and pulled in, brought alongside the Shepherd until we can hear His very breathing.

Every book we read, every sermon we hear, every broadcast we listen to in this condition is a bridge back to God. It is the call of the Shepherd into our sleeping soul. He has come to kiss us and bring us back to life with the kiss of reconciliation. The soul which is not restored is incapable of doing what it was created for – to glorify God and to enjoy Him for ever. You might take a book and use it as a door wedge, but it was not created for that. It was meant to be read. You can take a comb covered with paper and play a merry tune, but it wasn't created for that purpose. Lots of things are used in ways for which they were never created. Sheep were not created for loneliness and emptiness to walk alone through life. They were made to follow a shepherd.

The scene of the shepherd travelling with his sheep keeps changing. It is almost like keys in music – sometimes we find ourselves off-key. We need re-tuning! We need re-orientating. When the captain of a vessel needs to do that he studies his compass, map and other useful instruments such as a computer. In years past he would wait for the clouds to part and then he would take a reading from the stars. As he looked to Heaven he discovered where he was in the waters.

A Scots shepherd was asked: 'Will your sheep follow anyone? Will they follow another shepherd?'

'Only when they are sick', was his reply.

The love of God which is revealed to us in Jesus Christ and which constrains us, is always willing to start again. He makes all things new. He wants to be a Genesis to you . . . a Book of Beginnings, the Word of new hopes and desires.

The new life of God can appear as streams of quietness. It can be as oil flowing or grass of tender portions with a full cup. These can be metaphors of the life of God flowing through the believer who is restored. There are fresh pastures. You can go in and out and find pasture and food (John 10:9) . . . into a place where we can think, see, hear and know. Within the fold is far better than without in the fields. The peace His presence provides is far greater than the shadow or shade of an Everest. The Everest of His love is the Evermore of His Presence.

He 'returns my soul' is another thought in this phrase. It is returned to God. Those believers in Thessalonica had turned from idols to serve the Living God. This is not a negative turning or just an alteration in our position, it is the fact that we must turn to come home, to come to the Shepherd, to return into the area of hearing and obeying His voice. We have been as wheels stuck in the mud which need turning. It is not restoring for a better position but for purity and content to bring us among the flock so that loneliness is banished. He turns it from the shadow to the sun. He turns it from loss to the nearest, the deepest and the dearest, the Shepherd. The fulness of completeness is in Him.

Psalm 19:7 has the same thought of restoration in it. 'Converting the soul'. That word of the Lord is the voice of the Shepherd to the ear of the sheep penetrating the soul. It means not only to bring back – that would be the persuasion of love after poverty – but also to refresh, that is the supply and the loveliness of love.

God restores your feet to walk after Him. He restores your hands to work for Him and to worship Him. He restores your ears to listen to Him. He restores your eyes to watch for Him. He restores your patience to wait for Him. He restores your love to love Him. He restores your lips to speak for Him.

Tutankhamen had 365 servants – a different servant for every day of the year. God's sheep must serve Him like that. If a coin falls out of your pocket it goes out of circulation until you find it. It is lost from circulation. The soul which is lost is out of the circle of the deep love of God until it is found and restored, then it is put back into circulation.

'All we like sheep have gone astray' (Isaiah 53:6). We have vacillated. We have reeled under the burdens of life. Sheep are not built like oxen to carry yokes and pull ploughs; they are made to follow. One writer suggests the phrase could be read: 'He calms down my soul'. Hence the Japanese rendering of verse 1: 'The Lord is my Pacesetter'. As if we have gone like a runaway train or bolted like a frightened horse. A car out of control needs controlling. We have ridden and driven like Jehu racing alongside Elijah before the storm, but we need God to set the pace for the race of life.

You must pass through each verse of Psalm 23. God has to bring you to the reality of knowing verse 4 . . . 'You are with me' – in me, through me, around me as a fold.

A missionary was being shown the way through the jungle by

a native. The missionary, feeling hopelessly lost, asked: 'Are you sure this is the way? Do you know the way?' The native replied: 'I am the only way through here'.

Any shepherd will tell you what is meant by a 'cast down' sheep. It is one which has fallen on its back. It can never rise to go on without assistance from the shepherd. It lies there with its legs waving like flags, signalling to the enemy that dinner is now ready and the sheep ready for the taking! It has surrendered and its feet in the air are its flags of surrender. The shepherd searches for it and sets it on its feet again. This is being fully restored and experiencing a new standing before God, a new standing in God and a new standing with God.

A sheep needs rescuing from too much wool which gets matted and heavy, causing the sheep to be entangled in the thorns, bushes and undergrowth. It is there as 'woolly thinking'. We think we know best; our ideas, our knowledge, our intellectual attainments, the old life and the old nature all lead the sheep of God into trouble. It is Christ Who sets free to walk and talk with Him. We need to be restored, ransomed, renewed and righteous. It is only the restored soul which can enter the paths of righteousness which run into the House of the Lord for ever.

Six

He Guides Me in The Paths of Righteousness, For His Name's Sake

My Guide Into Right Paths

Once I have been restored and am walking along the Shepherd's chosen paths I can claim His guidance. Guidance always comes to believers when they are engaged in righteous acts of grace, love, mercy, peace and endurance – the paths which are right for us. There are right paths and there are wrong paths for us to choose. When we decide what is right we must do it in the shadow of the Shepherd and not in the shade of our own darkness. Divine leadership always leads along paths of righteousness and along the same way as scriptural truths. We may feel that we are walking along the sharp edge of a sword because it is so difficult, but the end of the blade is the shaft and the Hand of Jesus is there holding it.

Some paths lead to pain, to a precipice. We think the way we are going will lead us to a panacea for all ills, when in fact it only leads us into a place of weakness and restlessness. Some paths and some decisions we make lead into perplexity and anxiety. We can hear the hot breaths of the wolf and we feel we are walking on its teeth. Jesus never meant it to be like that. There is a confidence and a boldness in a sure way. God's paths are pure paths and they are also plain.

Abraham's servant said: 'I, being in the way the Lord led me . . .' (Genesis 24:27). The end was success. The true service resulted in satisfaction and execution of the Master's will. God's paths have always been right. The problem is to get us right and into those avenues of service and expressions of the love of God.

We are all journeying and it can be from Jerusalem to Jericho, from peace to that which has been roundly cursed. We can be on the Emmaus Road with Emmanuel and if we are then Jesus Himself will draw near and go with us.

The skill and manipulation of the Shepherd is seen in the paths that He is able to take the sheep along. The sheep may not see the reason why. The shepherd may be unable to explain the reasons; all he can do is expound the way before them and expect them to follow in his paths. The sheep always have the consolation that the shepherd goes before. He has travelled this way many times and been through many situations. The mellowed life is his and he seeks to minister this to the sheep. The Disciples never came to any place where God is not, nor have believers throughout the ages. When God led Israel He led them by the right way – the way which was right for them at that time (Psalm 107:7). It might not have been the shortest or easiest way but it was the right way. Whatever adds to our righteousness God will lead us that way, even though it be a hard way – The way of the Cross which leads us into the way of Christ. The word 'lead' (Proverbs 8:20, King James version) means to make to go on. Sometimes it is the need for food, at others the need for water, but at all times it must be in the paths which follow the shepherd. There is a high way, a lower way and a middle way. The right way means that at some given time there is only one way. Christ is that way. He is not a part of it, He is the whole way and nothing but the way. God does not operate by Father Time, He operates Father Time!

The paths of righteousness are as many as the branches from the vine. As the branch depends on the vine, so the believer depends on Christ and so the sheep depends on the shepherd. Every path is not just a few yards in length, but it is a path made up of righteous acts which stem from the One who wears the breastplate of righteousness. Each path is filled with many designs, many decisions, many actions, things which are weighed in the balance and only when the balance tips to that which is just and right can a path be taken. It is not any old path, it is the path of righteousness. 'To place your hand in the hand of God is better than a known way'.

The shepherd has been along these paths many scores of times. He knows where they lead and why He is leading in such a way. The Sodom of Lot may be the well-watered plain, but that which Abraham chose is more blessed of God (Genesis 13:11). It never had sulphur and fire rained on it.

God's paths are not barren. They are bathed in blessings which run out of a rock and trickle to our feet. They do not lead to a dead end but, if traced through, they lead us to a Living Lord (Revelation 2:8). The Bible leads us into no back yards or caves of crises, but deeper into Christ and His care which flowers along the way we travel. If you are led into the lion's den you will find the footprints of Daniel leading out. When we go into the fire we find the three Hebrew children have left footprints for us to follow. Righteousness is as the dream of Pharaoh and the dream of Nebuchadnezzar. It is all one. There are many right ways within right paths. Child of God, when faced with a decision balance it on your Bible, the whole revelation of the Bible and that which it contains, before you reach a conclusion.

In sign language we know that error is marked out by a zigzag, while a token of truth is a straight line. These paths are better than good intentions which the road to hell is paved with. If you want to discover whether a sheep is being shepherded, then discover which paths they are walking. God's paths never lead to empty houses, they lead to full cups.

One Puritan writer slices verse three of Psalm 23 into the following phrases: Gracious restoration, Holy guidance and Divine motives.

There is a pattern in the paths along which God guides and takes us in the form of a shepherd. The pattern for doing things is as true as the Nature of God Himself.

The Hebrew word for 'paths' is 'waggon wheels' of righteousness! Immediately it springs to mind that the way of the ungodly, in Psalm 1, verses 4 and 6, is likened to chaff which the wind blows away, and a path which disappears, found in the word 'perish'. Campbell Morgan states: 'The way of the wicked perishes, that is, runs out and is lost in the desert'.[2] One is a waggon track while the other is a disappearing track which you cannot follow. We have to place our feet behind the wheel which is moving alongside that which God is doing. This is the right path for you. Yet the word 'path' is more than just a track. It is a deep trench, well marked out and fortified, preserving us on both sides (1 Samuel 26: 5 & 7); it is a trench. If you want a refuge then hide in the pavilion of His righteousness.

Righteous paths are found to be favourable and we step onto them as we seek first the Kingdom of God and His righteousness. It is when we 'seek', inquire, desire and question (Matthew 6:33).

Paul said: ' . . . I have run the race, I have kept the faith.' (2 Timothy 4:7) I have kept to the markings along the track. I have played the game according to the rules and my rule book is the Bible. Win or lose, first or last, it does not matter. It is how we played the Game of Life. God's rules have to be our rules. The fruits of the Spirit must grow alongside these paths.

Even the Wise Men, after visiting Jesus, in Matthew 2:12, returned by another way. Seeing Jesus always takes us into and along righteous paths of purity. God counts the path right and He accounts those walking along that path as being right, the saints who are in Christ Jesus. They were saints positionally, saints potentially, but they had to prove that they were saints practically, not just sitting in a stained glass window. A saint is one who lets the light in, one whom the light shines through. To be saintly is to be on the paths of righteousness, seen in your walk, talk and your manner of life, to have holiness as clearly and crisply defined as a fresh wheel mark.

The word 'paths' is plural, even as the word 'waters' is. There is diversity and plurality in the Nature of God. New life breaks out all over in paths of righteousness.

These sheep were travelling along paths which thousands had travelled. The difference was that the shepherd was leading them. Aesop has a fable where the animal was hit by a piece of fruit falling from a tree causing its friends to say that the world was coming to an end and the sky was falling in. They were met by a fox who led them into his den.

In Rome, pieces of granite, slate and other materials were

placed in the pathways, telling of a famous victory in a far off place. The paths of righteousness tell of that most famous Victory on Calvary when Jesus Christ died. This path is worn smooth by the feet of those referred to as 'a great cloud of witnesses' in Hebrews, Chapter 12.

God never leads us into orchards that have no trees. God never leads us into righteousness and then expects us to be negative in our living. There should be righteousness running as a path from every house in the nation. On every motorway there should be a lane of righteousness! There should be such a path running through every house and from the front door to the garden gate.

There is an old law in Wales which states that every house must have two paths – one to the local well, the other to the local Church. This would really mean, nationally, 'Holiness unto the Lord'.

Sheep are creatures of habit. They would tread the same path for ever wearing out the shepherd's footprints and then guessing the way. That is why it says 'paths of righteousness'. In Zechariah 14:20, the day is envisaged when even the bells on the horses shall have Holiness written on them. If every shop bell had a ring of Holiness about it dealings would be along the paths of righteousness. If only every path could be a path of righteousness. One day, when He rules, it will be so.

The righteous are as the palm tree. The palm tree has over 800 uses. Righteousness needs translating into walk, talk, and on to the tongue to be sung. If Jesus is the Way, then He is the Way out of sin, the Way out of bypath meadows. He is the Way out of the grasp of Giant Despair. He is the Way out of error and sadness. He is the Way out of that worrying situation. That which is virtuous needs to be used in the very essence of society as salt. Christians must be as salt, as light and heat, in the fabric of society, not in some monastic cloister. The faith which fills with that right act, attitude and assurance. The rectitude of conduct is seen in Christlike acts. It is when we fill up the sufferings of Christ as we live day by day for Him. It is doing what Jesus would do in the situation, in the waggon wheel. It demands cutting across the field of human thinking. It is not going every way and every where, but going God's way. We need paths which are ever green for God. Paths which ever lead to the heart of the Shepherd.

The Jewish rendering of 'paths of righteousness' is: 'Unto the right paths'. As the round peg to the round hole. This is correct because God is always right, having all knowledge and seeing everything from every angle. That is why our word 'news' is made up of the four points of the compass – north, east, west, south. News from every quarter, seen from every point by the all-seeing Eye of God. Known as we are known by the knowledge of God. Loved as we are loved by the love of God. There is great strength in knowing that you are on the right path, and that path is one of equity.

Every path represents some attribute of our great God. In the early part of the Old Testament God revealed Himself to the Patriarchs by using different Names. Every path is a letter from the Name of Jehovah. Travelling these paths and making our own choices we discover the fulness of God, even as the sheep discovered the faithfulness of the shepherd. We come to the fulfilment of Paul's prayer when he prayed: 'That I might know Him . . .' (Philippians 3:10).

We have no need to be as the Indian scouts who had to cast dust into the air to determine which way the leaves had fallen or the way in which the twigs had been crossed. The astronomers and astrologers hold no secrets for the child of God. The only star we consult is the Bright and Morning Star. Jesus said 'My sheep hear My voice, and they follow Me'. Plodding the paths of God.

These ways always develop the sheep, they grow and they go. They mature as they munch. The sheep not only get to know the shepherd but the shepherd also gets to know the sheep. These paths are a revelation to the shepherd of the heart of the sheep. Every path was a crucible. Every path can be the Finger of God, changing, challenging, coercing – dealing with them in such a close manner He could minister to their minutest malady. These lands or paths were as our classroom; what they are to our learning and maturing they were to the sheep. The greatest safeguard any shepherd could offer his sheep was to keep them on the move. Straying sheep, sheep which will not follow, will soon be dead sheep. We must keep moving in righteousness. Our right standing must exceed back yard, back lane and the slippery slide of the unsure and unsafe. Paths: acting, walking, speaking, doing, with the ideal always before us. Jesus our Shepherd is not a dead marble or bronze model. He is a Living Saviour. We must keep our gaze on Him (Hebrews 12:2) letting our love flow to Him.

A path is a link between one landmark and another. The word 'path' in Luke 3:4 is a trodden path, a beaten path. The word given as path can mean to wear down, to rub as if rubbing corn in the hand. These are God's methods for your development. Our English word 'tribulation' is taken from the implement which was dragged over the corn to remove all the chaff. The word used for tribulation is akin to tero, tritum, from which we have the word 'trite', the word 'contrite' speaking of a humble, lowly heart.

There were parts in the rocky defiles and along the paths where there was only room for one sheep to pass. This is when the shepherd came very near. In the narrow defile there was closeness and oneness, there was a touch of tenderness as the sheep was helped individually by the shepherd.

In Hebrews 12:13 the straight path means a wheelrut. We then have the thought of running on such a surface, a track and a path. We have ongoing paths of righteousness. All His paths can be peace.

We are as much led of God when we feel the wheel is running over us as when we are being fed from the Hand of the Shepherd. Circumstances are no measure when measuring God's care for us. We are just as much at the centre of His will eating tender grass or drinking from a full cup, as we are by still waters. God arranges things so that those very things arrange me. They all blend together to make up the colours of life, which Christ seeks to place in our bland characters. The manifold, the many-coloured grace of God needs to come right into our lives. We must reject the words in the phrase: 'I am a wandering sheep. I do not love the fold. I do not love my Father's voice. I will not be told or controlled'. Paths of righteousness provide for us the very happenings which are going to control our lives. We may sometimes feel that these very paths are as the scalpel, cutting away the cancerous portions or the superfluous fat of Hebrews 12:2, given as weight.

It is not the expanse of the hillside or the mountain, the wandering and doing of our own thing, which develops us. Many times it is the ministry of the rod and staff along the way, the times when we are challenged by what is said and done. It is in the path that the Shepherd walks.

To find my life I must lose it. To win Christ I must turn other voices and other influences aside. I only recognise the paths of righteousness when I know that the Shepherd is there. That is why one of the Names of God is Jehovah Shammah – 'The Lord is There'.

Sheep must be more than wool, more than a bleat, more than a wagging tail or a frisky jump. There must be development. God isn't wanting to turn sheep into cotton wool, into coins or into statues, stones, logs or frogs. He wants them, as He does us, to develop into our full potential until we become the Lambs of God because of our personal association with the Lamb of God.

The sheep have their own brand mark on them, which tells of their owner. Righteousness stamps us, marks us out as Christian, Christ's man, Christ's woman – Christ's person and people.

A missionary visiting a Church was trying to explain the difference between the Islamic, Jewish and Christian Faiths. He said: 'Christians think in straight lines, whilst Arabs think in circles. Whenever you see two Jews arguing you will get three arguments! Jesus is the straight Way and the only Way to God. Radio may come to us along waves, but we need light to travel in straight lines'.

When the sheep commenced their journey as they developed from lambs they had lessons to learn through the things they suffered. C. S. Lewis said: 'God is shouting to us through our pain'. For lack of vision and want of leading, people perish. When a ship is nearing rocks the Captain looks anxiously for the light from the lighthouse. He seeks confirmation of course by computer and he constantly looks at his map to make sure of where he is. Many times when we face difficulty, as we do the

right thing, there are indications which will identify where we
are.

How can I find this righteous road? Remember the story of
Robinson Crusoe – how, in despair, he went to the old sea chest
and took out a Bible. That is the voice from beyond and the map
that we need. In that Bible is the way of comfort. The Bible cover
can be the very gate which leads into a way of sanctity. Christ
said: 'I am the Good Shepherd'. He also said: 'I am the Door. I
am the Way. I am the Life'. His examples enrich us, whilst His
acts inspire us, but His enablings mature us.

These paths are marked out for us in the Ten Commandments.

A woman lived with a man and she found his demands were
so great that she resented them and so she left. Later she fell in
love with another man and did everything he desired of her.
One day, whilst she was thinking, she realised that she was doing
for the second man the same things she had done for the first,
but this time it was not a burden. The reason? She had fallen in
love with the second man!

A woman read a book and thought that it was dry, dusty and
boring. Later, having met a man, she fell in love with him, not
knowing he was the author of the book. Then she read the book
again, and thought it was marvellous!

These paths are seen in the Beatitudes of Matthew 5 . . . Peace-
makers, pure in heart, the merciful, the hungry and thirsty for
righteousness, poor in spirit. Whatever they are, as in Matthew
5, they leave us in blessing. Happy are you. They are revealed
in the fruits of the Spirit – peace, joy, long-suffering, meekness,
temperance . . . against such there is no law.

There are those scholars who prefer the present tense . . . He
is leading me along paths of righteousness – as if it is happening
to David now and here. Not a past rut, but ploughing in a
present furrow. He leads me into that which is straight as an
arrow on target, rather than into something which is warped
and not true. Being true to God you will be true to yourself.
The way is straight. The word 'sincere' can mean that which is
uncomplicated. 'I have ceased from my wanderings and going
astray since Jesus came into my heart'. The path of faithfulness
is not to wander or meander, it is to follow Jesus.

It is all for His Name's sake. The shepherd's crowning joy is to lead sheep successfully along paths and through all dangers and to get them safely into the fold, that men might see His goodness and glorify God.

I mentioned earlier that shepherds had nicknames. Which Name would describe God in your life and on your pathway? It is likely to be because of this name that people will perceive, of a truth, that God is in your midst. Is He your Greatheart, as in John Bunyan's *Pilgrim's Progress*? Is He your Faithful? 'They beheld His walk'; 'they followed Him' (John 1:29–37). 'They beheld His glory' (John 1:14).

Every sheep which reaches the end of a journey brings glory and a glow to the Shepherd's heart. 'Rejoice with me for I have found my sheep which was lost' (Luke 15:6).

God wants to lead us into Redemption, Justification, Sanctification, through Reconciliation. He wants to bring us to our Father's house for ever.

Mrs Thatcher, a former prime minister, bought a new house, which she named 'Churchill'. We need to live where we are reminded of victories.

The early believers were called Christians because they went Christ's Way. They were called the People of the Way (Acts 22:4). A path or a way is something you have to put a name to. It is what you pass through and come over, without going under. Acts 12:10: Peter went out and on to another street.

John Calvin said: 'Unmerited grace will conclude what God has begun'.

Seven

Even Though I Walk Through The Valley of the Shadow of Death, I Will Fear No Evil, For You Are With Me

The Valley of Shadows of Uncertainties

Psalm 23, and particularly verse 4, is more than a collection of old bones thrown together, it is rather like flowers arranged in a garland of what has happened in the life of Israel's favourite King. It is the tabulating of a living exciting adventure with a shepherd. God has been writing on David's heart and David plays it on his harp.

There are those who thought that God was only a God of the mountains, the hills and the plains, not a God of the valleys. The sheep soon learn the value of their leader when they are in the midst of gloomy conditions and circumstances. He is always a step ahead of them, but not too far ahead to miss their faintest cry or the sound of an attack. Our God, as the Shepherd of the sheep, is a God of the sunshine and the shade, of the shadows and of the substance. He is the God of Sinai and of the Mount of Transfiguration, but before we reach that place we have to pass through many a challenge in a valley situation where we are walled in and cannot run away. God has to prove Himself in 'whatsoever state I am in'. I must find the glory of God in those situations. There are many means which God uses to mould the life and shape the heart. There were many deep defiles and narrow gorges which the sheep had to pass through and sometimes even their voices or their bleatings could become the dinner bell for some marauding beast to fall across their path. It was almost as if hell had spilled over into the valley, such were the terror and misgivings that these shadows brought to the mind of the sheep. These shadows and sometimes rocks which took on great shapes of magnitude challenged them to alter course and to run for it if they could. Pictures of torment and terror were suddenly thrown before their dim eyes as if an instant replay, but in the presence of the shepherd they had an instant reply! These dangers always drew the sheep closer to their leader, they were thrown back on the fact that their herdsman was with them.

They, with us, must learn to lean on love. Nothing which is formed against us shall prosper. He is the Defender, not only of our faith, but also our weaknesses and failings, seeking to turn those weaknesses into strengths and the failings into future success. They must be brought to a place of trust through trysting, not after the valley when they are back by the side of quiet waters, but right where they are in the valley itself.

We receive many gifts in life which have stamped on them the place of manufacture. God is stamping His sheep and saints and the difficulties we pass through tell us where we were made. Brush strokes are being added to the canvas daily.

Many of the noises they heard were just that – noises. They were the empty echo of a falling piece of stone and that which seemed to be as a caged beast in their imagination became a blessing because of the presence of the One who led them and brought release.

Jesus is more than a shadow, He is substance. He is the very substance of God, the 'expressed image' of His Person – the Character of God – the outshining of His splendour, the same substance as God (Hebrews 1:3). He is the Rock in a weary land. Jesus, the Great Shepherd, is the Refuge in a time of storm. The nearer the sheep were to the shepherd the greater the presence of that shepherd. 'Though I walk *through*' – they do come through – 'the valley of the shadow of death'. Job, more than any other writer, mentions the 'shadow of death'. Job 3:5; 10:21 & 22; 12:22 and 24:17 (twice). If death be like a shadowy hand then the living Hand of a Living Saviour is nearer and greater. It is warmer and surer than any hand of death. That hand of death has been robbed of its prey by Jesus Christ. The point of death which was in that hand has been blunted and taken away.

In the Book of Job there is a mine-shaft where can be found a vein of silver or gold. In that dark happening, Jesus Himself can draw near. There are precious things which we can discover as we allow God to uncover them on our passage through the narrow way.

The shepherd sometimes went ahead to check the well-known danger points and to chase away any beasts that could be a threat to the sheep. Jesus has done this in death. There is a light in the valley of death for the believer.

We have trusted God in green pastures, by pleasant and quiet waters, along the paths of righteousness, but now we have to learn to trust God in the difficult situations. We must realise that negatives become positives in the darkness.

It was after the Apostle Paul had spent a day and a night in the deep that some of his most miraculous happenings took place. Some of his New Testament writings contain such height, depth, breadth and length of revelation.

In John, Chapter 21, after the disciples had spent a night in the blackness, towing, rowing, reasoning amongst themselves on a failed fishing expedition, Jesus was seen in the light of another new day. It is what we pass through which puts into us what we are going to be throughout all Eternity.

Relationships between sheep and shepherd were bonded in the valley. It is the Shepherd being there which helps us to distinguish between figment and fig. He points out the real and the unreal, the difference between rock and rascal. The presence of the leader was more real in the dark than it ever was in the daylight. The shepherd now carried a particular lighted torch and its beams illuminated him in the dark for the sheep to see. As they walk in the light, as he was in the light, so the shepherd kept them from all wrong. We must follow and, after learning, commence leaning, trusting in the all-sufficiency of the Shepherd. He who has led us in will also lead us out. If it be into the lion's mouth – He can give it lockjaw! The hug of the bear can squeeze us further into the mould of God. The sweep of the eagle, those razor-like claws, can cause us to recline very humbly at the Shepherd's feet. Many times the lessons of God are written on a dark blackboard. Suddenly the green grass appears to take on a different colour in order that we might learn the things which God has to teach us. Every turn of the way and every valley is time spent with Mary at the feet of Jesus. You will learn more following Christ for an hour than all the learning of this world can give you in every hour of every day of your life. Our light afflictions work for us – exceeding weight of Eternal glory. That is worth a few valleys! That which God does cannot be weighed or measured. It can only be treasured in the heart, as Mary did in Luke 2:51. It can only be treasured on the trail and after passing through the trial. Dresden China has to be fired in the kiln many times before it becomes perfect. The best has to suffer the most. God's saints can never be statues or stuffed sheep, they are living, conquering beings, led by Him.

It is in the Valley of the Shadow that the shepherd becomes a living reality to the sheep. Getting to know Him through the valley. Finding the substance of the Shepherd in the shadows and echoes which surround us.

The sad thing about this particular verse of the psalm is that we have only associated it with death. We have put the undertaker's hat on it and built a coffin. We have formed a wreath from the words when in fact God is a God of the living. It should not be dressed in black, but in royal splendour because we are not left in the valley of death. Jesus did not stay there and neither will you. You can take a walk through a cemetery without being buried there!

For us to learn anything about the valley of the shadow of death we must notice the pace at which we come through. 'Yes, though I *walk*' – not skip, hop or jump, not even run. Walking speaks of faith, of peace, of assurance and of trust. 'They shall walk and not be weary' is the outcome of waiting on the Lord.

For our encouragement, to act as rod and staff, it does say 'walk *through*' – we do get there! Read the Book of Revelation and discover that ultimately we are winners. We get through because of His strength, His might, His power and His love – the exercising of His ministries on behalf of the sheep. It is because He helps us to distinguish between what matters and what does not matter that we arrive. There must be no push and rush when passing through the valley with God. It is step by step, moment by moment and hour by hour. Things which were not, are, and things which are, suddenly do not matter. He controls our pace, leading us to our place in God. He led Israel the right way.

If the sheep run through they can cause danger. An avalanche can be brought into the valley because of sheep running through and ruining the plans of the shepherd. Don't run away from day and into permanent night. Never run, for you will lose sight of the Shepherd. The avalanche of rocks will hide from view the One who cares for you.

If the sheep run, they will arouse sleeping beasts and temptations long since gone will return at the moment when panic holds its parade. 'Let sleeping dogs lie'. I must go through at walking pace, that He might sow in my heart all the things of love and the nature of God might have time to develop in me. If you run, you will sound the Charge of the Dark Brigade! The enemy at a distance will fly to your side. You can never outpace God.

As the herd travelled the jutting rock opened up like a child's storybook before them. The shadows took on new meanings. Everything in the valley appeared as something ready to spring out, as some jack-in-the-box, or released spring to conquer the defenceless sheep. That is why Charles Wesley's hymn says:

> 'Cover my defenceless head':
> 'Hangs my helpless soul on Thee':
> 'Leave, ah leave me not alone':
> 'All my hope on Thee is stayed'.

Pilgrim, in *Pilgrim's Progress*, came to this valley and from afar it seemed as if the valley was full of lions. When he came closer he discovered that they were all chained!

'They asked one another, "Who will roll the stone away for us?"' (Mark 16:3). When they arrived they found that the stone was gone. It was placed, like the graveclothes, in a place by itself. It had been rolled away!

The words in the Hebrew language have little to do with death. 'Shadow of death' is all one word in Hebrew and means 'dense darkness'. God has never promised His sheep death, but life. There is a future for all in Jesus Christ. The entrances to this valley are turned into the pearly gates of the New Jerusalem.

'Those who dwell in dense darkness, for them a light has sprung up' (Isaiah 9:2). That is a little bit different from beasts springing out and upon you, something attacking you from behind. When Pilgrim reached the valley the sun was shining all the way through it.

The reasons why temptations come and go and we have to pass through valleys is because Satan goes to and fro (Job 2:2). Temptations are only for a season. Manifold temptations are met with the manifold grace of God. Many wounds and stripes are healed in the diversity of the gifts of healing.

It is the presence of the Shepherd which breaks the power of every imagination (2 Corinthians 10:5), and casts them to the ground into an empty tomb to be buried for ever. John Wesley said: 'Best of all, God is with us'. If God is not with us, we shall not be carried forward. We all have our Emmanuel, operating in Emmanuel's land to fight for us. It is His presence which defeats the enemy. He is fully armed with rod, staff, stones, sling, and music from the reed, which itself has been rescued, after being bruised.

The pathway to glory isn't all glory. Neither is it all gory. It is a mixture of rod and tunes from the reed.

The middle verse of the whole Bible is Psalm 118:9: 'It is better to trust in the Lord than to put confidence in man'. The sweetest honey comes from Thyme, which is a bitter herb. God sweetens not only with a spoon but sometimes with shadows in the valley of shadows. Only that which is real comes out of the valley. The shadows never come out. They disappear with the sun. Only the Shepherd and the sheep, which are the real substance, come forth at the end of the valley. David came out of the valley of Elah with the sword of Goliath in his hand. No wonder, in future fights he said: 'Give it to me, for there is none like that!' Elah – meaning 'the oak' . . . from the acorn it can come forth. We can go in as saplings and come out fully grown, mature (1 Samuel 17:2, 19; 21:9).

When a class of young people were asked what was meant by the 'yoke of Christ' one of them gave the answer: 'It is when Jesus puts His arm around your neck'.

Listen to David: 'Thy servant slew both the lion and the bear' (1 Samuel 17:36).

And to Amos: 'Seek him that turneth the shadow of death into morning' (Amos 5:8).

In the King James version, up to this point, it has been a remote 'the' . . . 'The Lord is my Shepherd'. When entering the valley it changes to something a little closer. Now it is the more personal and nearer 'thou' and 'thy' . . . 'Thou art with me. Thy rod and staff comfort me. Thou preparest a table before me . . . Thou anointest my head with oil . . .' His presence and a deepening of relationship is found in the valley. His presence is found at the point of your need. Come around the corner and Christ will meet you there. The Shepherd has been going before the sheep. In the valley He is alongside the sheep. He takes up a new position for protection of the sheep. At the time and in the time of fears and shadows He draws alongside. 'You are with me'. That can thwart many attacks of the enemy. 'You are *in* me'. That can destroy all the power of evil which has come to destroy and to kill. It is said that when the bee stings anyone, it leaves its sting behind and is condemned. It has no more power to hurt. The devil stung the heel of Christ as that foot of Jesus gave a backward swing to dethrone the one who had been following and failing mankind. His power was surrendered at the Cross. Satan is a limited foe. Jesus is a limitless friend. Satan has lost his power to hurt. Jesus said: 'All power (including the power of Satan) is given unto Me in Heaven and earth'.

These valleys through which the sheep passed had different names, according to what happened in each valley. The history of happenings was written in the valleys.

Where I live in Manchester, a part of the nearby motorway is

named 'Death Valley' by the local people, because of the incidents and accidents which have happened in that area.

They were called the Valley of Shadows, the Valley of Stones, the Valley of Rivers, the Valley of Robbers, the Valley of Peace, the Valley of War, the Valley of Victory. By overcoming, we name our valley. The valedictory comes out of the valley as we come nearer to the Shepherd than we were when we entered. Through Jesus Christ a nameless valley or nameless experience receives a name. An empty valley is found to be a full one. 'You are with Me'. Like John the Baptist He fills every valley with His presence. His pastoral care is there unfolded as the sheep move along. 'With us' is an Old Testament expression. 'In us' is the New Testament fulness. 'In Christ' is found so many times in the Word of God.

'You are with me to comfort me'. A youngster wanted to be a Lion Tamer when he reached maturity. His teacher asked: 'But won't you be afraid?' 'No,' he replied, 'my Dad will be with me'.

'Teach me to live that I may dread, the grave as little as my bed'.

Revd Alexander Maclaren, the Scottish preacher, who thrilled people with his public speaking and writing, wrote: 'The Presence of Him who allows and sends sorrow is best able to help us to bear it'.

Matthew Henry, in his commentary on the psalms, wrote: 'God is a very present help in time of trouble. He is more present than the trouble'.

Always remember that Jesus is the Lily of the Valley and not only the Rose of Sharon's plain. He is not simply seated at the right hand of the Majesty on high, He is touched with the feelings of our infirmities. He is able to succour those who are tempted, placing His arms around them as they placed wrappings around a ship in a storm.

Paul records and recalls: ' ... The Lord stood by me ...' (2 Timothy 4:16, 17). As an officer standing by his soldiers, as the jailer stands by the prison door, so Jesus stands by us and stays by the gate. 'Under the shadow of His wing we find security'.

George Forrester has many monuments erected to his name. They are usually found in parks and gardens, and they commemorate the fact that he was a great explorer. He went on many journeys and made many remarkable discoveries. One of those was the rhododendron which he discovered in a valley in Tibet. There is that which God wants us to discover and uncover in the valley. There are beauties which need developing in all our lives. 'If only you knew what beauties lie in you', said Michelangelo, when looking at a piece of granite. What designs and destinies are yours in God!

In the valley we discover God, and God discovers us. Into our emptiness He places such a fulness which could never have been without our entering into the Valley of the Shadow of Death.

Eight

Your Rod and Your Staff Comfort Me

Comfort and Challenge in Every Crisis

There are so many situations into which sheep, if not led, will just wander. These circumstances prove to them collectively and as individuals the ability and capability of the shepherd. They open up his heart to them in rescuing missions, confirming that the sheep matter to the shepherd. All his training is witnessed in his reigning in every possible location. Wherever sheep are found, the shepherd is nigh to help.

When conditions arise which are not complementary then the rod and staff enter into that area of ministry which heals and helps those who have been hindered. Finding ourselves in many predicaments we begin to realise that at the end of the rod and the staff is the Shepherd Who is all heart. As the hammer is the extension of the hand, so the rod and staff are extensions of the abilities of the Leader.

The rod was used to beat off any attacker, while the staff was used to reach sheep which had failed or fallen into an adverse situation. What the rod could not reach, the staff could. The shepherd measured many distances with the rod and the staff before allowing the sheep to pass on along the way. The rod and staff ministered comfort to the sheep. When they could not hear the footsteps of the shepherd – perhaps because of a storm or swirling waters, the screech of an eagle – or the tune from the reed did not reach their ears, then the conductor of the sheep simply tapped his rod on the large rocks as he passed by. This was music to a frightened sheep. It brought jangling spirits back into harmony. When head and feet had no co-ordination then it regulated them. It told them that the shepherd was going before: that, although they could neither see nor hear him, he was alive and well. Those tappings of the rocks contained a message which every sheep was glad to hear. It was as the sound of the trumpet telling that victory had been gained.

When Jesus arose from the dead He tapped the stone and it rolled away. The Resurrection message is one of comfort for troubled and perplexed hearts. The Great Shepherd goes on in greatness and splendour. When adversity comes then Christ can rearrange the matter. A refuse tip can be so arranged that it appears as some botanical garden! We must follow Him, not in fear but in faith, not in trembling but in believing. Even if the way disappears into darkness it will reappear in a blaze of glorious light. You will be led into more abundant life.

One toss of the rod, thrown almost like a stone, was enough to send a marauder sprawling injured or dead at the feet of the sheep. The shepherd was so adept as to hit the assailant whilst at the same time missing the sheep! One smack with the rod was enough to send an enemy reeling in a gush of blood. Many an eagle has lost its grip because of the rod of the guide. Attackers were attacked with it. It was a fortress and a bulwark to the timid and shy lambs.

When a stone was thrown from the sling it was sometimes followed up with a crack from the rod. This was enough for any destroyer. It was beaten with many stripes. The herdsman could so throw the rod as to cause an avalanche and bury the victim; the terroriser was terrorised, the hunter was hunted – attacked by a rod.

It is the rod and staff, this two-handed ministry, which brings us through every Valley of the Shadow and on into the bright sunshine and clear running waters. We must let Christ help us to conquer every temptation. Every lurking fear must be put to the rod. Everything which would keep bouncing back into our lives must be put to the rod as a bat to a ball. It must be measured by His might.

The sheep could not assist in this situation. They could only follow on in the victory of their herdsman. They could only step over what he had trampled down. If any snake raised its ugly head then they came to a headless snake, the poison drawn from its bite because of the power of the hand which held the rod! When they were at some cliff edge or had fallen into a pit, the end of the crook was so shaped as to fit around the head and shoulders of the sheep. This crook was their lifeline. They were lifted back into the presence of the shepherd and into fellowship with other sheep as they were crowned with the crook, lowered into their situation.

The two ministries of rod and staff were quite opposite. The rod could and would knock off the feet, whilst the staff or crook would lift back onto the feet. Often the crook would be lowered under the middle of a weak, wandering lamb to lift it to the shoulders of the shepherd in order that he might carry it. A shepherd without a rod and a staff would be a dead shepherd. It meant that he had given in. The corrections of Christ prove that He is still working on our behalf, to lift us and draw us ever nearer to Himself. If we are without the rod and staff ministry then we are not sheep and there is no shepherd to deal with us. In another context, we are not truly born of God (Hebrews 12:8).

Jesus has not given in, or given up. He has gone up! He has gone before us, after passing through darkness and suffering, so that He might bring many sons unto glory. The Captain of our salvation has been made perfect through suffering (Hebrews 2:10). As a Man, He has entered the veil of human suffering, tempted in all points. The Shepherd had been where the sheep might find themselves. Even before sheep reached a ravine which, although narrow, had to be leapt over, it was measured by rod and staff. If they came to deep waters, those waters were first measured before the sheep entered into them. Everything we enter into, Jesus has entered into first. You can never move or fall into a situation where the Great Shepherd has not been. He has left the rod and the staff in Psalm 23 as a solid and future reminder and as an enhancement to all who find life's adversities difficult to handle. The University of Christ is not an easy one. We need the universality of Jesus and the circle of His crook to bring us through. A Christ less than a whole Christ is but an idol and a mockery. The Shepherd has the ability to deliver the sheep.

Jesus is not all rod; there is some grace alongside the grit in rod and staff. There is comfort as well as courage and challenge, administered by the Hand of the Herder and Deliverer. The rod and staff are bloodstained and sweatstained. They have many markings which bear eloquent testimony to the ministry in mastery of the Shepherd. Our trials allow the rod and the staff to enter and, through them, God brings us out into a reconciliation with the God we have wandered away from. 'All we like sheep have gone astray', we have wandered into many a lion's den, into and from the presence of the keeper of the sheep. Into deep and troublesome waters we have wandered. We, like sheep with our dim eyes have mistaken the saliva of the lion's mouth for the gentle waters of quietness.

The rod and staff were never used as exhibits. They were always carried with the shepherd and were part of him. In the New Testament, where ninety and nine sheep are safe and one has gone astray (Matthew 18:12 & 13), Dr Strong points out that the sheep meant to go astray. It intended to wander and to roam from safety, truth or virtue. There is the thought of our being deceived, as that sheep was deceived and led astray by the greener grass on the other side. Jesus Christ will activate both rod and staff where and when required. He moves in before I can move out. He moves into action – even when I am inactive.

We often speak of 'touching wood'. This action emanated because of the wooden ring worn by a King of England. If you requested a favour, you touched the ring and your request was granted. When the wood of rod and staff touches us it is to help us on to more certain ground and into the peace of the Fold of God.

The Rabbis saw the rod as the word of God. Jesus is called the Branch (Jeremiah 23:5; 33:15). This Branch bore fruit in sheep being delivered. They saw the staff as the comforts brought to us by the Word of God, the healing balm when we have been wounded by the world.

The rod is placed before the staff. The enemy needs to be

overcome; the temptation needs to be conquered before we can
be ministered to. Any surgeon will tell you that the wound has
to be cleansed by various methods before healing can take place.
The rod is the weapon of attack, whilst the staff is the weapon
of defence. The rod, or club, sometimes had a steel point at the
end. It had a nail as a point. The nails of the Cross can match
anything that Satan binds with. Jesus can nail him!

I heard of one lady in business who kept large nails in the till,
to remind her of what it cost for her to be delivered!

The rod is a symbol of the authority of Christ over every area
into which we must enter. The Americans refer to a gun as a
rod, because of its deadly accuracy when facing any foe.

What was in the shepherd's hands and hung from his side
'comforted' the sheep. It put new life into their old aching and
worn bodies. William Barclay, the great Bible scholar, writer
and university lecturer, points out that the word 'Comforter' in
the New Testament was used to describe a man who was called
into a situation of discouragement and whose job was to put
new life back into dispirited troops (John 14:15–17)[3]. There is a
picture, depicting the Battle of Hastings, 1066. It shows William
the Conqueror sticking a sword into the buttocks of the soldiers
and underneath the picture are the words: 'William comforteth
his soldiers'.

These weapons of warfare were meant to spur the sheep on,
knowing that the shepherd would see them through the situation. Take heart my friend, the rod and the staff are available
to you, but they must remain in the timing of Christ. There will
be a moment when you require that which has been kept close
to the Shepherd's heart, as the rod and the staff were, to deal
with your situation. The word 'comfort' means to breathe easily.
That is what God is able to do for us. The hearts of the sheep
were not beating so strongly that they could leap out of their
bodies. They drank easily, they fed easily, they followed easily
and, because of ministry, they walked out of misery.

Like John we need to lean on the Lord's bosom and breathe
easily (John 13:23). This leads to sleeping easily. That is the place
of Jesus in John 1:18 . . . in the bosom of the Father. 'Comfort me'
– 'You comfort me on every side' (Psalm 71:21). As if wrapped

in wool even as the sheep are. It is as Jacob was comforted by the news that Joseph was still alive. It is not the sheep being chased, harried, worried or falling and being dashed to death, but it is resting after rescue on the shoulders of the shepherd or in the fold, with the leader and master as the doorkeeper.

Henry Martyn, the missionary, said, 'While the Shepherd lets me see the rod and the staff, I am comforted. God in action leads to my reaction of resting peacefully, knowing that all is well. The rod and the staff can clear the grass or the valley of hidden dangers. I must trust in His triumphant grace'.

Your rod and staff they comfort me, they refresh me – ready for another day, another journey, another step towards my goal which is God Himself. Not pain, not reason or joy, but God, desiring Him as sheep desire green grass and still waters.

John Trapp, the gifted Puritan commentator, writing on this rod, states: 'Like Moses' rod, it sprouts and blossoms again; like Jonathon's rod, it has honey at the end of it; as Ezekiel's rod, it measures us'. It is the measure and more for manifold temptations.

The verb 'comfort' is in the future. We have a future in God and a comfortable future, knowing that He will take care of us. It was the memories of managed crises which brought relief to the sheep. Not one curl of wool will be sheared from your back without the knowledge of your Heavenly Father.

Paul refers to God as the God of all comfort. The place of relying on His strength is the place of comfort and joy. Without Christ there is no easy breathing, only a gasping for air, not knowing if your next breath will be your last.

Psalm 4:8 says, 'I will both lay me down in peace and sleep'. Wrapped in peace like a blanket, sleeping soundly and safely in the Saviour! Oh, what comfort! 'For Thou, Lord, only makes me to dwell in safety'. He gives His beloved dreams in their sleep.

Our own word 'comfort' is made up of two ideas: *Come*, to bring together, to come alongside, to come and be a partner; and *fort*, a blockade which is built around us and where we have the figure of the soldier in the fort.

Let the intervention of our good and glorious Great Shepherd be turned into a convention, a true comfort to us whether on mountain top, in the dell, or in a dark situation.

Nine

You Prepare a Table Before Me in The Presence of My Enemies

Feeding on His Faithfulness

Jesus Christ is food for thought! Everything about Him is nectar. It is on Him, as the Living Bread, that we are fed now and evermore. Whatever battle in life we face we gain as we think on Him, as we are with Him, hear of Him, respond to Him. We are strengthened by feeding on Jesus Christ.

Jesus, when doing the will of God, said, 'I have meat to eat that you know nothing of'. When we fall into line with the Divine will our plate is a full one.

Whenever we come to the Sacrament of Communion we feed on the blood and flesh of the Lord Jesus Christ (John 6:51 & 53). There is drink and meat in Christ for us as sheep, even as there was a table prepared before the sheep by the Shepherd. The content of the cup, the courses, and the arrangements at the table are with Jehovah Jireh – 'the Lord will provide'. 'I shall not want'. It is a matter of knowing, of receiving and of doing the will of God which becomes almost like that which is edible and enjoyable.

I am reminded that our word 'sacrament' is taken from the very word that was used by a Roman soldier prior to going into battle as he took an oath to be true to Caesar and to all that was Rome. It was an oath of allegiance, seen in the word sacrifice. We feed on His sacrifice, even as the high priest fed on the carcase of the offered animal and received his portion from the flames. We receive something from the sufferings of Jesus Christ which is as food to the spirit.

As we feed on the bread and wine at the Communion Table we are doing as the shepherd did for the sheep. As we feed on the Emblems we are embellished, and endurance becomes part of us. There are those who will never understand what the believer sees in Christ. 'You are fair, my love'. When feasting on Him through faith, He becomes our Heavenly *manna*. The meaning of manna is – What is it? and while some are questioning and debating we are enjoying the pleasures for evermore (Psalm 16:11). The pleasures are those things which are pleasant and sweet. Psalm 81:2 describes the music of the harp. Song of Solomon 1:16 describes the pleasantness of Jesus Christ. The shepherd knew the individual tastes of his sheep, but Jesus Christ meets every need. The menu for our table is in the word of God. I can order, but the Shepherd does the arranging.

There are certain requirements which sheep and the Christian worker or server needs. The Shunammite woman in 2 Kings 4:10 provided such for Elisha the Prophet ... a chamber, a bed, a table, a stool and a candlestick. The shepherd, for the sheep, provides a chamber in a fold, a bed in a green pasture; a table is provided, a stool as a place to rest or sit, and a candlestick in the guise of the shepherd himself to enable the sheep to pass through the valley with a glowing torch. Through the bare necessities of life God provides the fulness and the diversities of New Life. Not all at one sitting. You cannot fill one plate, one cup or one table with it. There are many sittings in grace.

Onto this table, provided by God, there are many delectable items for us. The provision is so great that the table is too small. My mind cannot take it all in. There is so much that one thing has to be positioned on top of another. Special shelves have to be placed under it. I begin to realise the largeness of my Father's hand and heart, that He has bread enough and to spare. That which He fills is filled to running over. The quiet waters, the tender grass, the goodness and mercy, the cup running over are all without measure. 'Exceedingly, abundantly, above all that we can ask or think'. It is more than mind can comprehend, more

than the caverns of mind can store, and more than tongue can
tell. It is that which I cannot measure with my tongue . . . I cannot
get my tongue around it to pronounce the fulness of Divine
supply. There is no bleating here, only eating, as satisfaction
overcomes fancy.

The table which the Shepherd provides is measured by the
number of the sheep. We can fill the table, or allow God to fill
it with things from His Word. Here there can be for us the water
which was turned into wine, the bread which Jesus multiplied,
the honey which Jonathon tasted spread on the manna from
Heaven. We can have meat to eat which the world knows not
of. This food does not meet the need of gastronomical juices, it
meets the deep-seated requirements of my spirit, poured into
it from the table of provision. If you are too weak to partake,
then God can break the Bread of Life and the pieces can be made
to the size of your mouth. If God has provided then it will meet
your need. To be seated, satisfied, satiated is a glorious thing in
Jesus Christ, for we are 'seated with Him in Heavenly places'
(Ephesians 1:3; 2:6). There should be no thin kine among those
sheep following the Shepherd!

The sheep were so close to the shepherd that it did not matter
who or what was watching, they were fed out there in the
wilderness. The ravening wolves and the birds from above were
kept at bay by a presence stronger than metal fences and more
real than a closed door. We feed on the love of God, and John
3:16 becomes an absolute feast in itself to those who believe.
When we begin to meditate then Christ begins to mediate –
between table and mouth, between desire and drink, between
the edible and the enormousness of the love of God. Turning
over and over in our hearts all the things which God has done
for us we rejoice in these things more than in the time of the
harvest of wine or in winning the battle and taking the spoils.
What animals do in chewing the cud, we do with what Christ
has accomplished for us, in us and is seeking ever to fulfil
through us. C.H. Spurgeon used to speak of turning truths over
in his mind as a sweet should be turned over in the mouth,
rolling it over and over with the tongue.

As that food is transformed into wool and horn with hoof and skin, the work of Christ is transformed into Holy Christian living, until we live, act and journey like the sheep of God with the Shepherd. These sheep are well bred, well fed and well led.

It is a spread table in itself just to know that I am known of God, that God knows me and I know God. That knowledge will continue as long as the grass grows and the still waters flow, and as long as wool grows on the backs of sheep.

Paul, in Romans 8:37–39, is convinced that whatever enemies are around us they cannot separate us from the love of God in Christ Jesus. Of all that the Shepherd had and was, the sheep received their share.

Christ is food for thought as we think on His life, on His death and on His Resurrection. As we think on His Holiness and on His Second Coming, all are a basket of food for us. 'For me to live is Christ' (Phil. 1:21). Paul ate Christ, slept Christ, drank Christ, thought Christ and felt Christ.

The best shepherd provides the sheep with the best food for the best reasons and in the best place – right where they are. Manna might fall as dew and quails fly from above, water gushes from a rock, and the saints, as sheep, are well fed. Christ in this wilderness of a world is made unto us wisdom, righteousness, sanctification, redemption (1 Cor. 1:30). He is the Bread of Life, the Water of Life, the Life of Life. He is sweet to the taste, harmonious to the ear and glorious to the gaze. The Rabbis tell us that when the Manna fell from Heaven it tasted just as the Israelites required it to taste. To the hungry soul every bitter thing is sweet. In the hunger, the bitterness is removed. Desire is a transformer of feelings and food. It makes whatever comes palatable. It stamps every vessel on the table: 'All things work together to them that love God' (Romans 8:28). That working together is pieced together through our love for God. Everything is synchronised to the purposes of God. It works as musical instrument with musical instrument, until the whole symphon-ises together. Those happenings as the sheep travel along are taken and used by the shepherd. They become instruments in his hands. The enemies around are used to defeat the enemies within. The stone which fell from the cliff above is now placed into the sling, ready for the next attacker. That which attacks sends the reticent sheep running to the shadow of the shepherd. That which hurts provides more trust.

In the wilderness a clearing was made for the sheep and whatsoever provisions the shepherd could find were prepared there for the sheep. They were eating, whilst the shepherd was watching. He, standing by them, was their safety. Most animals are at their most vulnerable at water holes or whilst grazing. 'The angel of the Lord encamps around those who fear Him (Psalm 34:7). He sets up his tent around them to keep them. The Shepherd is where the sheep are, and the sheep are where the Shepherd is. He opens His hand and satisfies the desire of every living thing. That satisfaction is there even before the hand commences moving or working to feed.

Do you remember the wall plaque that used to be in most Christian dwellings: 'Christ is the Head of this home. He is the silent listener to every conversation'. Wherever and whenever you sat for a meal, that simple statement of faith greeted you.

The text states, 'You prepare a table *before* me'. God does not want us turning back to be fed on yesterday's food or the cabbage leaves of the last or latest crisis . . . the faded flower of what God has forgiven and forgotten. We must not be as the proverbial dog, turning back to its own vomit, or the sow wallowing in its mire.

The grass is only greenest on the other side when we are on the wrong side! The advert in the antique shop – 'The best present is the past' – is not true in this context. The very word 'sheep' means to go forwards. It is the sheep going ahead, looking ahead, who receives that strength through food from the hand of the Shepherd. I have not seen the righteous begging bread, baking bread or breaking bread. God is providing it in plenty. The granaries of our Joseph are filled with the capacity of Heaven.

There is always more ahead for those who are travelling with the Shepherd of the sheep. There are scenic views and the delights of Canaan stored up in the heart of the Great Shepherd, and the sheep becomes a part of those things. He wants to lead them and lay them down in what is in His heart. His thinking, His deciding, His choosing and their following leads them to eating, feasting, drinking at the table prepared. Sometimes it has been a long time in preparation. Jesus doesn't simply say, 'Give ye them to eat'. He provides what He intends us to have. There is deeper thought put into feeding sheep than was ever placed into the formulating of a great banquet. Lots of Churches have exuberance, but when the parcel is opened and the food comes out it can be very little indeed.

'Verily thou shalt be fed' (Psalm 37:3, Amplified Old Testament). 'Feed on his faithfulness.' ' . . . Feed on the bread of affliction . . .' (2 Chronicles 18:26). 'Feed on the bread of tears' (Psalm 80:5). You will be fed on oil and honey with the heritage of Jacob. God would feed us. Not all at once, but here and there with a little. Not with crumbs of comfort, but with loaves of love. On this table is set all the righteous acts of the Lord. God can feed by a miracle in the wilderness. The pot of oil and the cruse of oil. The ravens of Elijah's story land on this table. 'I shall not want' finds its true fulfilment on this table in the wilderness. There are almonds from the rod of Moses. There are waters of refreshment just to be near to Christ. There are many at this table. All are bidden to the Gospel feast. There is Lazarus, here the blind, the lame, the deformed. The man with the withered hand is eating with two hands! Those who would, like Mephibosheth, hide their deformities under the table have no need now. The wine jars from the Wedding of Cana stand in the corner! The man from the Gate Beautiful does a dashing waiter service! The ointment from the alabaster box still lingers in these areas as we feast on our freedom in Christ. 'My God shall supply all your need'. As you have given, so it shall be given, pressed down, shaken together and running over. Like the Disciples on the Mount of Transfiguration we would wish to dwell here for ever. It is good for us to be here, to drink deeply from the wells of salvation and to enjoy the bread, with enough to spare. The hymn (The Lord's my Shepherd) puts it very beautifully: 'My table Thou hast furnished, in presence of my foes'.

God has prepared it for us, even as the shepherd has prepared for the sheep. The prepared table is greater in abundance than the presence of the enemies of the sheep or of our souls. For every blow of the enemy there is a cup of comfort. For every snarling lip and threatening tongue there is a supply of grace.

For the echo of voices and the mutterings there is the clear, concise Voice of the Shepherd. The enemies are only a presence and will pass away, but the provision is for ever and is substantial. In the preparing of this table there is an exercise of Lordship over all foes, over all enemies, over every fear. There may be fire, but it will not burn us. There may be lions, but they will not kill us. The eagles may swoop, but they ascend with empty talons, grasping only the thin air. They take frustration, not food. In their grasp is not even a crumb. They cannot handle well-oiled sheep! The only thing they receive is a bolt from the blue in a blow from the Shepherd's rod!

What David enjoyed as a pilgrim refuge (2 Samuel 17:27–29) we can enjoy. Barzillai brought that food which David required. There is such a long list: bowls, bedding, articles of pottery and items for those articles because they were thirsty and tired. The sheep had a feast whilst the enemies had a fast. The answer to temptation is to feed on Christ, the Living Bread, not the dead loaf of religion. Get so big in God that the enemy cannot lift you and carry you away. Get so close to Christ that, to remove you, the enemy would have to take Christ as well!

He has prepared food for us. All we have to do is to open our mouths if we are hungry enough, and He will fill them. Sometimes we do not receive because we are not under the table in humility (Matthew 15:26,27).

The whole tenor of the word 'prepared' is so meticulous as to arrange an army. Strength goes in at the mouth. The weak are made strong at this table. The sad are quickened with Holy joy. The tired find that they have new life. Those whose feet have been turned out of the way are turned back into the ways of the Lord. The weary and thirsty, the fainting and hungry have their needs met as the Vine lowers the branch to where they can reach, or the wind blows the fruit falls at their feet.

You 'prepare', to set in a row . . . row upon row of that which you need. As Holy Bread upon the table (Leviticus 24:8) . . . which David and his fighting men came to eat (1 Samuel 21:6).

The same preparation for this table was found in God advising and commanding Moses to make articles of furniture for the Tabernacle. Worship is important, and God sees that those longings are fulfilled. After a period of travel, inducing weakness or tiredness, there was no sight greater to the sheep than when the Shepherd provided good things. It meant another break in their journeyings, just as the green grass and still waters did. There was sacrifice involved in the making, supplying and preparing of this table. What greater sacrifice can we have than Jesus Christ, Who laid down His life that we might go in and out and find pasture? That the will of God might become part of our daily diet? Jesus laid Himself down so that He might become the table from which we eat. He lies as low as is necessary for the sheep to reach the food.

A table spread like this was, like any feast, a sign of welcome, of honour, of privilege, acceptance and gladness. The sheep became the shepherd's adverts for the food.

This psalm and verse is the answer to the question in Psalm 78:19: 'Can God furnish a table in the wilderness?' The answer is Yes. As we go through this world you will find that, for the sheep of God, there are tables prepared and set out by God Himself at intervals, just when we need them. God did it for Israel. He did it for Joseph in Egypt. God can do it for you. A table prepared, and the sheep eating, means that the enemy is at bay.

The word *companion* is a compound word: *Com*, meaning a friend who comes alongside you, to be with you on every side. The river can flow away and the green grass can fade away. He has said, 'I will never, never, never leave you'. *Panion*, to eat bread with a friend, one who goes with you and eats bread with you. This is what a table prepared means.

Ten

You Anoint My Head with Oil

Touching Where It Hurts The Most

The sheep are cut and bruised by many a fall. A slide can soon develop into a slip, causing a fall. When the sheep stumble and fall they bruise, and damage is done which has to be repaired. Even as they seek to stray there is the sharpness of the thorn which would cut them open, and infestation occurs. The bush can be a handful of knives cutting into the sheep as it passes by. The ragged rocks claim their wrecks in sheep which are branded deeper than with some hot iron in the branding process. By the scarred tissue you can tell where the sheep have been. There is a lot of healing work to be performed and quite suddenly the table becomes the operating table as sheep have their infestation brought within the fold of the Shepherd's all-seeing eye as He applies His knowledge and experience. A sheep can be a ball of sores. Its experiences have caused its limitation. It cannot follow as closely as it should. It is limping. It cannot see as it should. It is lingering and is in danger of being destroyed. It needs to come close to the side of the herdsman. Suddenly, what seems to be a bundle of ragged wool can be helped and newness of life can crawl from that matted mess. How many times in the New Testament did Jesus leave them clothed and in their right minds? How many times did Jesus send forth His judgement unto victory? If the sheep are going to travel on then the wounds have to be cleansed and oil has to be poured in as a saving grace to further the rapid healing process. This oil, like the Holy Spirit, acts as a balm as its healing qualities become instant anaesthetic. There are healing virtues in the anointing. It comes as the out-stretched Hand of God to arrest corruption and bind with many bonds. Wounds which are ragged and torn, wounds which control the whole body, can be controlled by the oil. One drop, a few drops, are enough for large tormenting sores. The oil puts serenity into sores. Every drop is the death knell for parasites.

This is not just superficial healing. The deepest healing was when the sheep's head surrendered to the oil. The shepherd with the oil reached parts that water or anything else could not reach. This oil washed from within. It cleansed within. It operated in an entirely different sphere from water or wine. The oil reached parts that other things did not even know existed. If the wool would hide, then the oil would seek out, uncover and heal. Matted wool and human excuses are poor plasters for healing.

Sheep receive new legs, new eyes, new ears; all things are made new by the anointing which flows from the cruse. Jesus is the Cruse. 'I will baptise you in the Holy Spirit . . . I will pray to the Father and He will send the Comforter'.

The psalmist claimed that this oil should be his portion (Psalm 92:10) – For a fresh wound, a new hurt or a misunderstanding. The only thing which will cushion a fall is the anointing oil of God. The sheep knew that if the shepherd was close by and the teeth of the marauding beast had done its evil work, the stench of the wound would be nullified by the aromatics which oozed out of the oil. The very essence of the oil would freshen the tired and wounded limb. The shepherd gave something to the sheep which would not make it dull or restrict it. It would not become as another burden.

God is able to do the same for you, believer, through the grace of the Holy Spirit.

When the Greeks and Romans entered into combat, their skin was anointed with oil. Specifically, in a boxing match, or a wrestling match or where they were to meet opponents at close quarters the oil did its work. Their shields were anointed as they went into battle. This made the shields more difficult for the enemy to handle and consequently more difficult to overcome.

The oil gave them another layer of skin and it became as armour in the battle of life.

We all need fresh oil to keep our walk with God fresh. We need to be sacrificing until the sweet savour and aroma proceeds from us (2 Cor. 2:15).

The cruse which the shepherd carried was kept full to overflowing. It was the hurts, the needs of the sheep, the injuries sustained by the lambs that the oil flowed to. It was his hand to their hurt. His hand to their chaffings and their needs. The plenty was poured into their pain – the measure that was to bring them pleasure. They received the exact amount according to their suffering. They held oil in a wound. The oil will not simply fill the wound, it will heal it. If the work is of God and the Holy Spirit then things will be different. The ministry of the Spirit is that you might be one whole new man in Christ. All our injuries, all our battle scars, can be covered by the gracious influences of the Holy Spirit. The One who prepared the table will pour the oil. The One who healed the sick, the blind, the deaf, will anoint us with oil (1 John 2:27). The anointing of the sheep was according to need. The anointing of the Spirit abides within. He is always there, as a Shepherd watching over the sheep. Whenever an attack comes and at whatever hour, the Spirit of the Lord will raise up a standard against it. Whatever the size of the situation, whatever its similarities to that which has happened before, there is enough power in the Shepherd and the anointing to meet the needs of the flock. The oil flowed to where the hurt was most felt. Its commission was to seek and to find and to stay until healed. He is the Eternal Spirit with endless influence to meet endless needs. When we come to the end of ourselves and our resources we come to the beginning of the Beginning. We need the sure anointing from the Cruse of Christ.

An artist was studying some reproductions of a famous painting. He commented: 'If it is not real then it is not valuable. If it is not valuable, then it is worthless'.

The anointing is real and valuable! God pours His best into us to make us the best possible. He makes us precious. He can crown your cuts and bruises. The Name Christ means The Anointed One. Christians first received that name at Antioch

(Acts 11:26). There are those who feel the name refers to the anointing we have received from the Holy Spirit. It meant and does mean not only a follower of Christ as a sheep, but the anointed ones or a 'Son of oil' (Zechariah 4:14). The Shining Ones. Having the Glory of God shining from us like Moses, who had to cover his face (2 Corinthians 3:7). Our light shines from the soul.

Due to the grazes and the deep cuts of the sheep, because of the holes in their flesh, the oil was poured in and as the target was reached, so the sheep was healed. The Holy anointing oil given through Christ comes because of the wounds in His Body. The shepherd poured the oil into the wounds as liquid healing. The Holy Spirit is poured into hearts because of the wounds of Jesus Christ. The promise of God (Luke 24:49) is the cruse from which it must be poured. As you believe, it is tilted with the move of love and flows into your heart, whereby we cry (not bleat) 'Abba, Father' (Romans 8:15). We have the same Greek word for the sending forth of Jesus (Galatians 4:4 & 6) as is used to describe the descent of the Spirit, not in dove form or as water, but as oil. Here, oil was the need. As Jesus was sent, so the Holy Spirit was sent (Luke 24:49).

Guests, to prove they were welcome, were always anointed. The Spirit proves us to be more than sheep, more than soldiers; it proves that we are sons of the Living God. What the seal was to the sack or the letter found in Ephesians 1:13, the anointing was to the sheep. It was a mark of their worth. The shepherd's oil was precious. He did not pour it onto wolves, or rocks or bits of old stick; it was reserved for a purpose. The moment we move through the New Birth and into the purposes of God, then the Holy Spirit begins to be poured out of and into us. As we move near to the Shepherd, so the anointing is poured. The Spirit of God will always glorify Jesus, and when we are close to Him, born of Him, then the Spirit will rest on Him and bless us. The deeper the wounds of the sheep, the deeper the penetration of the oil. The greater the longing and need we have of God, the deeper the work of the Spirit.

The work of the spirit, the anointing, is to 'convict' mankind. 'They were cut to the heart' (Acts 7:54). They were dealt a blow in their hearts. They were stabbed through (Acts 2:37). The sword of the Lord had done its work. They were sawn as they listened, but to those who repent, the anointing oil of the Spirit flows into that aching void. There is sometimes a cancerous growth in the wound which has to be sliced away by the Spirit. The rose almost begins to grow on the dunghill as the oil begins to flow. The Prince is certainly seated there. The sheep could come as a bundle of sores and leave with the assurance that all was going to be well. It could be as Job, smitten from head to feet, but each part of each wound was dealt with by an open eye, an open hand and an open cruse.

We need the balmy influences of the Holy Spirit. Our word 'scruples' comes from the fact that small irritating particles of sand get between the toes and make them sore, causing irritation. From this we obtain the word scruples. We need oil pouring in so that we can walk as Jesus walked, so that, as lambs of God, we can walk like the Lamb of God. We should walk as Jesus walked and then we would talk as He talked.

The Spirit is given to Jesus without measure (John 3:34). It is a measure without length or capacity, a cup with no brim and an anointing without a cruse. God did not grant Jesus the anointing of the Spirit from a thimble or a ram's horn. You cannot measure the work of grace in the heart but you can measure the work of the Spirit by the source of the Spirit. Who can tell what God has wrought in lives and hearts? Commencing with the Book of Genesis these testimonies glow with the anointing, and in the Book of Revelation they are still going forth to conquer, as if from a womb which is involved in continuous acts of birth. Eternity, which is no small place, will be filled with those who have received a measure from the Immeasurable.

Which shepherd could ever measure the healing virtue of a drop of oil as it fell into the wound? They came as small hospitals, as surgeries, with a cure. The enemies which had nestled within were soon aroused and commanded to leave. Any Lazarus in corruption, who stinketh by now, will be loosed and let go. Any foreign body which has made a home in the flesh of the sheep is attacked at its place of attachment.

If the ears of the sheep became infested then the sheep could not hear properly. The same applies to the eyes. They are usually quite dim, but termites can bring blindness, so they can neither hear nor see the shepherd. These things need dealing with through the anointing.

A flock without sores and not out of sorts was a testimony to the shepherding abilities of the shepherd. Happy indeed are the people whose God is the Lord! Where Lordship reigns there true healing takes place. What is scarred and marked, gored and gashed, is garmented in grace. God does not poke the hurt. The Proverb states: 'Probe not an old wound too deeply'. The leader of the injured never asks where they received such a blow, but heals the hurt of the heart. The anointing oil is flowing, healing, warming, soothing and tender as it stitches flesh together again with the gentlest of needs. The Chaldee paraphrase, is: 'You have anointed with the anointing oil the head of my priests'. Those involved in sacrificial acts were anointed. This anointing always brought refreshing joy, that is why the smearing of oil stands for joy. It suggests a people who have been set free and are enjoying that freedom, running as readily as the oil ran down Aaron's beard right to his collar and to the bottom of the garment he was wearing. There is length and depth in that which the Spirit rubs in. How gentle, how amiable, how able is the anointing! Making every scratch its patch and every pain its plain!

There are three main attributes of oil: smoothness to the touch, like liquid silk; brightness to the sight. That is why we have oil paintings. Fragrancy to the smell. Sweating bodies were cooled by it. The works and the energies of the flesh are met in the flow of the Spirit.

'My *head* You anoint with oil'. It was the head which needed cooling. The hot and angry head, the anger, wrath, clamour, need the oil. It is that which penetrates woolly thinking. It was through the mind that Eve was beguiled (2 Corinthians 11:3 NIV) ' . . . Your minds may somehow be led astray from your sincere and pure devotion to Christ'. Nothing should come between us and the Shepherd. It is the work of the Spirit to formulate and maintain that work of Christ within us. The head and the heart need the flowing over of the Spirit of God. We need to be like the Grecian shields which were anointed with oil before soldiers went into battle, so that every sword might slide off, every spear thrown glanced away. Everything the adversary throws at us is met in the daub of the Spirit. It strikes the Spirit first. It has to penetrate the anointing before it can touch us. The anointing shall break the yoke. It will loosen it. It will wither it. It will fray the temptation until it has no strength at all. When the yokes are of iron, there is that slipping through and out by that which the Spirit supplies (Isaiah 10:27).

We can all have within our heads that which is as wooden as the Horse of Troy and which can be our undoing. Through the Spirit there is a wooing and a welding together in strength. When we have been split asunder by the happenings of life the oil can piece us together again. Bone can come to bone and flesh to flesh, back to where there is wholeness and oneness. He takes my weaknesses and pours oil onto them and they stand up as strengths before the onslaughts of the hostile.

Jesus is always our Example. He received the anointing of the Spirit. Jesus of Nazareth was anointed of God and went about doing good. He did not just go about. God the Father had sealed the Sonship of Jesus with an anointing (John 6:27). In the Old Testament the lamb which was placed on one side for the sacrifice had a seal placed upon it. John the Baptist refers to this in John 1:32–34, when he saw the Spirit descending on Jesus Christ. As the lamb was sealed with a particular seal, so also when the Spirit rested on Jesus He was sealed, anointed by God. He is the Lamb of God. He is called the 'little Lamb', the Lambkin (Revelation 5:6). Twenty eight times in the Book of Revelation He is called the 'little Lamb'. We need to become as tender young lambs, following Christ into every experience.

C. H. Spurgeon said: 'A dead creed is no good. We must have our creeds baptised in the Holy Spirit'. Without the Spirit they will become infected and disease the whole body. There is a living death without the influences of the anointing oil. We need something to cover our hurts and to administer healing within that covering which will not allow them to re-surface. We need to plant our pains into the promise of the pouring out of the Spirit of God.

When they looked for sores and infestation, all they came

across were patches of oil, placed there by the tender hands of their leader. As the shepherd called them to his side he called them by name. When the anointing is received then a new new name is written down in glory and it is mine, mine.

When flesh did not reach flesh because of lacerations, then the sheep needed that which would bridge the gap and pull the two severed parts together. When joint was not in line with joint, the oil was needed. There is no schism where He is Supreme. There is a tremendous unity in this anointing of God through Jesus Christ. There is a piecing together as a puzzle; the pain and the problematic are pacified. Drops of liquid love parcel up sores of all sorts. Every drop of oil had the cancelling of the injury of the animal. What a difference between the anointing oil, smooth, easy, velvet relaxing, when compared with the razor-sharp teeth or paw of the lion and the bear. How gently it ran into the open wound when placed alongside the swooping eagle with its outstretched talons and open beak swooping down and falling upon the lamb as a stone from the skies.

The sheep have been on the dusty path and have gathered all sorts of termites on themselves in the open sores. The herdsman uses that which is soft and gentle in oil to meet with the hardest and roughest treatment. There is ointment in the treatment. The sheep, before commencing a new journey, need a new anointing to refresh them. That journey, or any journey, must commence with the hand of the Shepherd and the oil flowing from that hand into the wound. With the oil on your head you can meet things face on and conquer. The oil meant that the Shepherd was close by.

Eleven

My Brimming Cup Runs Over

The Fulness of Capacity

If everything I have written about Psalm 23 was brought together the cup would be full and running over. There are moments in God when we are overwhelmed by His goodness until our cup overflows. All the drops, day by day, have been entering into this moment and that which we taste has been fermenting for us as the years have passed. The cup is shaped to fit the head of the sheep. As we gaze to drink, we see our own image in the contents reminding us of all that which God has accomplished for us, in us and through us. That, and that alone, makes a full cup and one that is running over.

That cup is a mirror of good things, pressed down, shaken together and running over. Each blessing is not a sinking but a sailing vessel. As I gaze into a full cup my image, the reflection I see, cannot alter the course of the contents. Those contents are not spoiled by what I see of myself or in myself. I am over-whelmed when I see the hand of the Shepherd reflected in every drop.

Fanny Crosby, the blind American poetess and hymn writer, wrote:

> 'With numberless blessings each moment He crowns,
> and filled with His fulness Divine,
> I sing in my rapture Oh Glory to God,
> For such a Redeemer as mine!'

The very word blessing, used so many times in the Scriptures, can mean a pool of water. When we seek to review the blessings of God down through the years, step by step with Jesus all along life's way, through the valleys and over the hills, with green grass and stilled waters, it is like counting the sheep or numbering the shells scattered on the seashore. Paul often referred to the riches which are ours in Jesus Christ: Riches of His grace (Ephesians 1:18); the riches of mercy (Ephesians 2:4); riches of glory (Ephesians 3:16). All these are combined in the one phrase, 'unsearchable riches of Christ' (Ephesians 3:8). The word 'unsearchable' means not traced out. The King in his Counting House counting out the money cannot count out, spell out, write out or reason out the blessings received in an overflowing cup. You cannot count them, you cannot follow them through to the end. If books had to be printed then the ink would run out when trying to assess, accumulate or accentuate the blessings of the Shepherd in the cup which is placed before the sheep. It is like starting to count today and to be still counting a billion years from now, and having as much to count as if you had just started! The blessing in the full cup causes it to run over. You cannot trace out that which runs over.

These are fresh contents running over the sides of a cup daily, and hourly. It is repetition, but as with snowflakes, each one has a different design. As we meditate we turn them over and over. The mind and heart become the full cup. After a while we realise that the half has never been told.

The cup full and running over means that neither yesterday, today or tomorrow will ever be the same. The same cup, yes, but a different portion is being poured into it by the Shepherd of the soul. It means there can be no stagnation for the sheep. There needn't be any two days the same. Nothing should be flat but everything should be as fresh as an overflowing cup. There is an inflowing and an outflowing in the Christian life for all.

His Righteousness, His goodness, His leadings along paths of righteousness bring you to the place where you overflow. Things which have happened to you are pushed over the sides of the cup, to allow new things to come into your life. Like the Kingdom of God, there are things in it which are old and new. The sides or the size of the cup does not matter, but the multiplicity of blessing received does.

Satan would place a lid on the cup. The fears of fox and wolves would do that. A shadow would flit across the top, but with the Light of the World by your side the contents would still be seen. The lion's paw would cover it or one of the rocks could roll and cover the top, but in this psalm that does not happen. It is an overflowing cup.

The cup 'runneth over' (King James version), 'Overflows' (NIV version). Dr James Strong tells us that the word 'runneth' is from a root word meaning 'satisfied'. 'To slake the thirst'.[4] To drink deeply of the things of God and at the Fountain of the Spirit causes the cup to overflow. Psalm 66:12 has the same inference, a wealthy place, that God has brought us to saturation – as saturated with satisfaction as Gideon's fleece ever was (Judges 6:38).

When I awake in His likeness, I shall be satisfied. The pure in heart shall see God. We can see His likeness in an overflowing cup; that Godliness can be seen in what overflows the life of the believer which can be cup-shaped and cup-filled overflowing. The reflected image of the Shepherd is also seen in these waters as He stands close by. The needs met are seen in this cup that overflows. As one thing flows out and leaves the cup, so another new thing takes its place. What a life is ours in God! God floods lives, He does not feebly attend to us! The cup is at once a fountain head and a stream with a river running through the midst. It is well supplied. It is a full provision, projecting past, present and the future in an overflowing cup. Note that the cup is not overturned, as a challenge, or as if giving in. The cup is not hung up. There is no plea for it to be filled. As a matter of course, if sheep follow the Shepherd, the cup will be filled. It brims over with blessing. It overflows with the ongoing purposes of God. It is not a pouch or a bottle; they would be difficult for the sheep to drink from. It is standing as an open barrel. There is an ongoing here. We need to be full as a cup which is overflowing with the blessings of God. Even our clouds should hold waters and fulness which can be used to glorify God. This is the cup of echoing memories and majestic happenings. When we come to the full cup we come to a waterfall and we feel like the youngster who saw a waterfall for the first time and asked: 'Can we stay here until it runs dry?' Or maybe like the child who, coming to the seaside for the first time, ran from the bus straight to the sea lest the tide should go out and it should disappear for ever!

This cup is not full to overflowing in every verse or at the bend in every lane we travel, but now and again the overwhelming goodness of God does its work in the soul.

It sometimes seems less full than at other times. That which God empties and cleanses He also fills. He fills lives with His life. Promises fulfilled are like cups running over. Mary felt this when she spoke the Magnificat (Luke 1:46 onwards): 'My soul doth magnify the Lord'. Simeon's words are in the same vein (Luke 2:29 onwards). So many are content with a shallow cup, one that does not run over the sides. The dregs will do for them. God's will for us, as the shepherd's for the sheep, is that we might have a full cup running over with the blessings of God. Our thanks to God and our praise should be measured in a full cup which is overflowing. 'Here's my cup, Lord; I lift it up, Lord; fill it up, Lord; fill this longing and thirsting of my soul'.

During their journeys the sheep are deliberately brought to a place where the mountain streams have flowed into holes, holes which are full and running over. It is to these that the sheep are brought for refreshment; waters as the snows of Lebanon melt and freely cascade, meandering down the mountain side into a dust bowl to place within its perimeter this kicking, living, refreshing water. That barren bowl of dust is to be transformed by water which runs into it, just as your life can be changed by the Water of Life. That tired, tied and tasteless tongue of the sheep, sticking to the roof of its mouth like some dead Lazarus, is called forth, and as a fish entering fresh water it is revived. It is baptised in fresh and refreshing waters. All its lost taste is returned through the water. This is what God can do for you. It is a cup of water given in the Name of the Shepherd to thirsty sheep and it does not lose its reward. God is able to fill all ceremony with fresh water. Our empty laughter and joy can receive its escaped nature again. It can be brought back. Those who have hung their harps on the willow trees can take them down again as we sit by these waters. They are as tasty as taste itself. They are fresher than fresh. They are without price, without endeavour. We may come and drink as the memory is flooded, as flooded as it was in the days of Noah. As the deer pants for these waters, so we pant after God until a fulness is reached. The greater the longing, the larger the cup, the more it overflows. These overflowing cups may be just around the corner. Another day or another hour and it will be so for sheep and shepherd. All the trials and hurts, the wrongs of the journey, swim away in an overflowing cup.

During the days of the Soup Kitchens in London the advert went out: 'We will fill a vessel with soup, if presented'. A woman arrived carrying the largest jug anyone had seen! She could hardly lift it, but, according to the promise on the poster, it was dutifully filled with soup and with the help of her children she carried it away.

Do you remember the first trickle of the love of God into your life? God wants to add to that until it becomes a portion, then a cup, then overflowing! The overflowing is in the knowing of the Shepherd. There is depth in the cup and an overflowing besides. We do not impoverish the cup of salvation by drinking from it, we add to it! When we take, God's reply is to replenish. We can never take more than He can give. We can never out-give God. He has given more sun than we can enjoy, more stars than we can see, more sky than we can measure, more seas than we can fathom, and more contents of a cup than we can ever drink. The woman at the Well of Samaria, in John 4:28, left her pot because she had obviously found a much fuller source, a water which would spring up into Eternal life (John 4:14).

The waters of Shiloh run through this cup. Part of the waters of the Jordan and the Red Sea run over the brim, speaking of the fulness of the activity of God. The waters on which Jesus walked are here. Moses and all his miracles are here: Moses, meaning 'drawn from water'. All the uses of water are here. The miracles are overflowing the sides of the cup. Only Jesus can turn your water into wine!

One translation states: 'My cup shall be full'. There is a confidence of full capacity. My Father has water enough and to spare. The confidence of a full capacity, running over. It is referred to as *my* cup. It is a very personal and individual thing. God can make it happen for you. Tip out what is already in your cup, get rid of the loose stones and the dust and let the Spirit of God flow into you afresh. You will overflow into a thousand tributaries! What remains stuck in the bottom can flow out and through the inpouring there can be an outpouring. If it is real and comes from above it will not cease at dew or moisture, but will go on into the flow of running over. The sun will not smite it by day. It will not wither because of lack of moisture as in the parable (Luke 8:6). It will lack neither moisture, depth, height, breadth or length. Every word of testimony given is an overflow of the cup of God's caresses to the soul. The overflow is the ongoing purpose of God for the life that the Shepherd has brought them into. The sheep have not gone out alone as water diviners to find it. The waters have been brought to them and they have been brought to the waters. There are special times when parts of the puzzle fit together, when lip and cup meet along the way. The things of ceremony and of religion will not meet the need of thirsty sheep.

These overflowing cups are the 'amens', 'Praise the Lord' and the glories of new life in Christ. When Elisha raised the young child a sure sign of life was his sneezing (2 Kings 4:35) – seven Ah-mens at once! God wants us to receive more than sneezes. There has to be an overflowing out of an overthrowing. When Moses smote the rock, there was a real overflow of water (Numbers 20:11), but because of the smiting of Christ *my* cup can be 'filled to overflowing'.

There must be something of the overflowing cup about new life in Jesus Christ. That is why they ran to the Tomb (John 20:4). Zacchaeus made haste. Romans 12 speaks of being fervent in spirit. There must be that desire and that zeal which runs over even as a cup which receives greater than its capacity. You never know when the cup is going to run over (Ephesians 3:20) 'exceedingly', over and above all that we can ask or think: more than tongue can tell or mind can comprehend. In this cup is joy unspeakable and unforgettable, even unthinkable in its immeasurable capacity. This portion of the cup is immeasurable and that is why the penman, in Psalm 16:5, writes: 'The Lord is the portion of my cup'. Measure God who inhabits Eternity and whom the Heavens cannot contain, and you will have measured the cup which is overflowing. Jesus Christ emptied Himself (Philippians 2:7). This was the Kenosis of Christ (Philippians 2:7); he 'made Himself of no reputation' – 'Emptied Himself,' (Revised Standard version). The self-emptying. Emptied Himself of all but love. That is some emptiness and some fulness! He who was rich became poor that many might be made rich. The riches of His grace reaching to all the human race.

Joseph saw to it that Benjamin had five times as much as anyone else (Genesis 43:34). At the conclusion, in Genesis 45:22, Benjamin had five changes of garment and 300 pieces of silver. We have and are receiving so much of His grace. All we have in an overflowing cup is the down-payment. We are waiting for the Fountains of Heaven. If this is just a part, then what will the fulness be like? If this is the shadow, what then the substance? On each, even the immeasurable is measured when compared with the fountains of the life of Heaven. When the enemy comes like a flood then the Lord will raise up a standard against him (Isaiah 59:19). The enemy knew that when the standard was raised, the opposing army were moving out to war. Flood him out! That is how to get the victory! Fill the cup, not with the failings of feebleness, but with the victory of your faith which overcomes. Fill it to overflowing, not with your doubts and fears but with your demonstrations of delivering density. If you have a full cup it is a loving cup. You are not seeking water from broken fountains, you are depending on the Lord. When the cup runs over it drowns the enemy of the soul. Dirty devils do not like clean refreshing water! They can't walk on water, they sink as a stone. They go to the bottom of the river like a well-laden chariot. Even those around us who would try to master us, get stuck in the mud.

It is not a Christening we need, or a sprinkling, but a baptising until the water is in the cup and the cup is in the water.

We are not drinking from a leaking vessel or as a baby from a teat. 'I will pour out . . .' (Acts 2:17, 18). The same designation is given to Jesus as He pours out the changers' money from the tables in John 2:15. God will pour into your capacity. God will operate in the pressed down, shaken together and running over. God's measure is always to pour and to pour as if that which is being poured from is leaking, but it is not. It is just so full that it wants to fill every cranny and crevice of our hearts with that which is from God.

These waters in this cup never find their own level, for they are full and running over. You can never put 'full' or 'finished' on the works of God towards His children. There is no end to this drama; there is no finale in this measure of life, for you even carry the happenings of earth into Heaven. That which God gives is not as some embellishment. He doesn't wrap cups with ribbons for presentations, but fills them to overflowing with something that is alive, running, spilling, racing, flowing for ever! There is no measure you can place on anything which is provided and given in this psalm. Even the rod and the staff are not measured. The Shepherd's capability is poured into my capacity until it runs over and over and the cup is lost in the contents. To be lost in God like that! Just like Moses was. As the people passed by all they saw was the hand of God, not Moses. He was hidden in the cleft of the rock as God passed by. He was covered in the shadow of the Almighty (Exodus 33:22).

Twelve

Surely Goodness and Mercy Shall Follow Me All The Days of My Life

Mercy as Much and As Often as Required

The happy life, the contented life, the progressive life in God is a well balanced life, made up of goodness and mercy. If we are going to ascend, it is by these two helping us. If we are going to run with God, it is on these two feet. Going through the valley, on to a path of righteousness, by green grass or to a cup filled until fulness seems an emptiness compared with that which God is pouring into it, is because of goodness and mercy, these delectable twins which come up from behind as the Shepherd leads us.

To some, these are the very first things they knew when they came to Christ. After you have known God's goodness and mercy once you can be assured of them for ever. They are part of, 'I am the Lord and I change not'. They are with us and are ever travelling towards us as the unchanging elements all the days of our lives. It is goodness and mercy which make us part of the flock. It is goodness and mercy which lead us alongside and to the side of the Shepherd. It is goodness and mercy from commencement to conclusion. All that we are and ever will be is written into these two words. Whatever happens, be it in darkness or in light, you will find buried in that knowledge, these two things, goodness and mercy as the two wheels on the waggon tracks or pathway. They follow us all the days of our lives, moving as those two wheels, filled waggons sent by God with glorious provision and help. Like Jacob we rejoice when we see them (Genesis 45:27). Every trial, every dark cloud formation appears that these two might operate in our lives.

Usually you would think about goodness and mercy going before us, even as the shepherd goes before the sheep. No. The Shepherd is before, the sheep are in between and the goodness and the mercy follow. Here is a threefold cord which temptation, be it valley or plain, cannot easily break. With the Shepherd leading, goodness and mercy gently nudge us forward. In a sense there are three shepherds leading the sheep – one before and two bringing up the rear. They care for every sheep as if that sheep was the only one. When the sun shines it ripens the apple until it beams out its red colour, as if it were the only apple in the world. Since they operate from behind us, goodness and mercy keep the same pace as the slowest of the sheep. If we are more dashing, then they are also. Whatever our temperament they temper it with His loving kindness and tender mercies. Many times we do not see the need for these two but it is in times of trouble, in times of danger that they are most needed, to rescue the perishing and to care for the dying. We do not need the aid of God until we come into certain situations. Goodness and mercy are the rod and the staff which defend us and lift us out of many a terrible situation. It is goodness and mercy which lead us back onto straight paths. They help us to live lives as straight as the barrel of a gun. Wherever we go or wherever we have been, goodness and mercy have followed us in, up, on and through in order to bring us out.

There are those sheep who are weak in sight, sound, limb and wind and who will struggle behind at the end. They particularly need the goodness and mercy of God to help them to keep up with the rest. It is the goodness of God and the mercy of God which calls us on, takes us on and sees us through every situation. The New Testament translation of goodness and mercy is the Grace of God which is bent towards us. God reveals His grace through the good of His glory and the mercy through His might. God is into forgiveness, and this includes goodness and mercy in a big way. Were it not for the grace of God, there go I – there am I – but, because of the grace of God – HERE am I. I am what I am because of the I AM!

When we are found lingering and weak, He is also there, travelling alongside those who are wandering, in order to bring them back into the way. Even when we fall, we find the Everlasting Arms allow us to fall only so far. It is the goodness of God, not the Shepherd's rod but His goodness in the staff which lifts us out of situations and takes us on into revelations. Every path is strewn with these. They prevent us and they pasture us. It is this which leads us to repentance (Romans 2:4). After we have been in contact with the goodness of God then it, too, has a full cup which is poured into our lives through the mercy of God. When we have a correct impression of the goodness of God then mercy flows in healing virtue to every heart. You cannot have goodness without mercy. Goodness leads you back and mercy carries you on. These two are the starting and the finishing line for the Christian.

One little child, on returning from Sunday School, told her parents that she knew the names of the shepherd's dogs – Goodness and Mercy!

These twins operate with the sheep of God, moving through every overflowing cup and growing with every blade of grass. They are found in every valley, they form the hedge along the paths of righteousness. These two are clearly heard in the call of the Shepherd and they are found in the tunes which come from his pipe as he plays on it. You cannot make the Shepherd all good without making Him all-merciful. One works with the other. Like rod and staff they operate together. When we see the Shepherd we taste goodness and mercy for ourselves. They follow us along the downward path. They go with us to the edge of the cliff. As in life, so also in death. They *remain*. They are the abiding influences of the Shepherd. God's sheep are branded with these two words, not simply as words but as working words which mean something to the sheep. It is goodness and mercy which carries the lambs on their shoulder. It is goodness and mercy which lights a light in the Valley of the Shadow of Death. As we pass through we see that lights have already been lit so that we might see our way through. Someone has been here before. It is goodness and mercy which sees us through and goes through with us. There is more comfort in these, more strength in these than in the rod and the staff.

Jesus went about doing good, but He went in and out among sheep after He had seen them as sheep without a shepherd. He was still thinking of sheep before His Ascension when, in John 21, He said to Peter: 'Feed My lambs'. It is goodness and mercy which are found helping, healing, keeping.

There are very few things which operate from behind for the Christian. They blow as some fresh wind over straying steps and blot out the fact that the sheep ever strayed from the Shepherd's side. Goodness and mercy blot out the mistakes of yesterday and heighten the blessings of bygone days, transforming them into greater and brighter tomorrows. What are our tomorrows in God? Simply our yesterdays which were empty, filled with goodness and mercy! What tender grasses to lie down in, with the sweet smell of Heaven and the aroma of that which is to come, that which awaits us, not as the snarl of the open-mouthed wolf, but as the smile of the Shepherd at the end of the day. All things do 'work together for good' to them who love God (Romans 8:28). God sees that all that we pass through becomes a fellow worker, a help in time of need. God does not operate in the singular but in the plural – goodness and mercy, well balanced, coming to us from above and below, from right and left. The words 'work together for good' are found in Mark 16:20 – it is the same Greek word here given as the Lord 'working with' them. In James 2:22 it is used of faith which labours alongside works.

Isn't God marvellous! He is so thoughtful . . . goodness and mercy shall follow me. There are past pains and paths which we have walked which have not been pleasant, but goodness and mercy have brought us to where we are today. There are pools of filth which goodness and mercy turn into a cup which runs over. It is only when the cup has run over that we begin to realise our lifestyle in God. There are many times when we do not realise until after the event that all things worked together for good to those who love God. As we pass through it is darkness, but when we arrive at the other side we look back on that darkness through light, and that makes it altogether different. Only then do we realise that goodness and mercy, as wool on the back of the sheep, have been with us all the way. Sometimes you can look on the reverse of a Cross that has been stitched in wool and you cannot make out what it is. When you turn the material over you see the Cross clearly, and something that was a puzzle, the Cross has made sense of. The suffering of Jesus sanctifies our suffering. The same applies to Romans 8:28 . . . as you consider the stitches at the back of the cloth, all you have is the shape of a cul-de-sac, seemingly leading nowhere, but when you turn it over the words are clearly visible (Romans 8:28): 'All things work together for good'. God places them in His goodness and feeds them to us in His mercy. All the discordant sounds He takes and tunes into a symphony of His love.

In Exodus 15:23–25, when they came to their bitter Marah, it was the wood cast into the waters which sweetened it so that they could drink. Many times, honey flows from the carcase of the lion. What began as an ordeal, because of goodness and mercy, has caused honey to flow out of the difficulty (Judges 14:9).

When we get into the Eternal House of the Lord we shall understand just how much goodness and mercy was spread out in angels' wings and how much God spread on our daily bread. 'God, our help in ages past, our hope for years to come.'

You must always see God as good before you can know His mercy. The rich young ruler came to Jesus and Jesus tried to point him to the goodness of God by asking him about goodness. This would have led on to mercy (Matthew 19:17, 18). We can only call God good when we have seen His goodness and mercy in operation. The Holiness of God is not altered by the compassion of God. Jesus did not have to lower the standard to meet the need. Jesus Christ was and is both the standard and the need met. Goodness at one place, mercy at the other; and need met – with 'shall not want' in between. These attributes of God are not wedged into a time or limited in their application. That is why they mean so much to us today, 'all the days of my life'. Every day is touched and tinged by some truth as we travel and are tested. Number them by goodness and mercy. Count them as the stars shine in the Heavens and as the grass grows below. I don't have to keep looking for them, shouting to them or seeking them out. My responsibility is not to keep dragging them along or hoping that they are with me. 'They follow me, all the days of my life'. Whatever life is, whatever the dimensions or length of that life, then goodness and mercy will be there – at the beginning and at the end. When we come around Wit's End Corner on to our knees, they are there to lift us back onto our feet.

Where I live in Lancashire there is a row of houses or small cottages. One has the name 'Wit's End', whilst another in the same row is called 'Woodland View'. Why the difference? They both stand overlooking meadows and woods. If you are following your wits or your intellect then the way you think will lead you to that cottage, 'Wit's End'. Following the Shepherd as one of His sheep will bring you, through goodness and mercy, to many a 'Woodland View'.

If you want two guards on your train of life then here they are – goodness and mercy, taking me through, seeing that I don't come off the rails, signalling me through life. This goodness and mercy of which the sheep speaks always travel behind. That is where I need these double, deft and durable ministries the most – behind me, where I am blind. The things about me which even my closest friends will not mention. We all suffer from spiritual BO – blind operations, bad objectives, base objections – and we are conscious of none of them because they are behind us. Precisely where we need help, in our blind areas, that is where these two graces operate. Goodness and mercy will deal with these. We all have our blind spots, but these twin helpers cover them all as we travel on. Goodness forgives them and mercy covers them all.

These two kindnesses which produce glories act as gate keepers. The sheep simply wander through that which is open. It is goodness and mercy which close every gate for security. They close the gates tight shut on all the past years. They make sure that we go in and out. If God has forgotten the past and clothed it in goodness and mercy, then why must I bring it to remembrance? If God has cast it into His sea of forgetfulness, why must

I have my little tea cup from which I read the past? This is not an excuse for sin or fault and failing, but an enrichment and an encouragement to Holiness. What mercy needs, goodness supplies. That which goodness needs, mercy yields. What is never found in quiet waters and tender grass is found in goodness and mercy. It is not an occasional action but a permanent record of the Shepherd's dealings with the sheep.

The reason we need the goodness and mercy of God to follow us, providing that double covering, is found in Ephesians 6:11–18. In all the God-given armoury of the Christian soldier there seems to be no covering for the back. That might have been simply because the soldier was not expected to turn his back to the enemy or run as if afraid of the conquest. With sheep in Psalm 23, it is quite different. Their backs are covered with goodness and mercy and it is a well constructed covering, constructed by the Architect of the Ages! Well might we say, if it was not for the goodness and mercy of God and that double covering which has followed us all the days of our lives, where would we be?

These are the two doors into the greenest of pastureland. These two are the pastures in which we need to feed often. The more we taste, the more we partake, the more there is. There are many 'daily' things for us in the Scriptures which are bound up in goodness and mercy all the days of our lives. God is not one thing, or two things, as found in goodness and mercy. God is not many things to the believer. He is ALL things: daily rate (2 Kings 25:30); daily teaching (Matthew 26:55); daily Cross (Luke 9:23); continuing daily (Acts 2:46); and daily bread (Luke 11:3). Goodness and mercy are there to see us in, to see us through and to see us travelling on for ever.

Goodness merges, and is intertwined, with mercy. We must know goodness before we can appreciate mercy. Where does goodness cease and mercy commence? Where does mercy commence and goodness cease? The answer is, with God. Goodness holds open the door, and together they act as that which binds us closely to Christ as the sheep are bound to the shepherd. Goodness and mercy are not static things, such as a frozen lake or a statue. They are not moulded in marble, cast in bronze or seen in slate. They stand not as rocks to be passed by. They are following, moving, ministering servants of the Shepherd. These words are not carved into a tree trunk. They are targeted on me. They follow me all the days of my life. They run with me, skip with me, rejoice with me. If I fall or stand, they are with me. They are the clear windows which I can gaze through at the pleasantness of God's paramount provision, standing not like hills but like twin mountain peaks as testimonies to the goodness and mercy of God. Goodness is where God has blessed me. Mercy is where God has revealed Himself to me. These two act as altars which have been erected along the way. They are as the stones which the patriarchs used to erect as testimonies to the goodness of God in the land of the living. These have become my Mercy Seat.

Goodness is the word which is found elsewhere as beauty, pleasant, precious, pleasing. Ecclesiastes states, 'everything is beautiful in its time'. So it is. Everything which comes from the hand of the Shepherd to my mouth and into my life is of that order. It is an Eternal dispensation and an hourly sensation, goodness and mercy. Goodness describes the well-being of Israel (Numbers 10:32). It goes on to record the well-being of a slave with a good master (Deuteronomy 15:16). It is the word used to describe how Saul's heart felt after being troubled by an evil spirit, when he heard the sweet music of David trilling from the harp (1 Samuel 16:16 & 23). These two harps of gold standing in the torn corners of my heart. When I don't understand what has happened or what is happening, then goodness and mercy are following and will be revealing themselves into the situation almost like a fish leaping out of the water. In the Christian life we have mercy every moment of every day. It is our waking thought and our sleeping sweetness, as it is in every verse of Psalm 136.

Mercy is found in love or loving kindness. David could say: 'Your gentleness has made me great' (2 Samuel 22:36) – as if the very path along which the sheep travel is the love of God. The steadfast love of God never ceases. Like goodness and mercy it never comes to an end. The God of Israel neither slumbers nor sleeps.

This is a revelation of the Shepherd's faithfulness as revealed in mercy. Mercy is great acts of deliverance and rescue. God has rescued you from more things than your mind can understand. We only recognise certain times when God has rescued us, but what about those many times, as many as the blades of grass, that we don't know of? I am reminded that the word 'rescue' in the English language, is taken from the Latin, and means 'to shake out'. Not to make out, or simply to shut out, or even throw out, not even to bleat out, but to 'shake out'. God shaking us out of situations into which we have allowed ourselves to wander. God shaking us out, taking us out, bringing it about by His mercy. Shaken by mercy – what a lovely experience!

In *Pilgrim's Progress, Part 2*, Christiana took with her one called Mercy, who accompanied her on the Christian way. We need mercy at every bend in the road to conquer every hole in the hedge. When we have no water to drink and no grass to taste, then we can throw ourselves on the mercy of God. It is as large as God Himself. Mercy is that which bows the neck, even as Jesus did when He died on the Cross, exhibiting universal mercy and its might through the Cross (John 19:30).

What a standing is ours! What a station we have in life! What salutation attends our every move as the sheep of His pasture! In ancient days sheep were referred to as those with the golden hoofs, because of their value and benefit to the shepherd. When counting the riches of a man, the sheep were his coinage. We are His workmanship, His poetry, His writing, His Creation (Ephesians 2:10). Created in Christ by goodness and mercy! There is more of it in the life of the believer than there is wool on the back of the sheep!

There is a special role in which the rearguard of an army functions. It has to divert all attacks. It delays the attacking forces, it lays traps for them, it dissuades them, it brings them to a halt, whilst the army in front marches on. The mercy and goodness of God in Christ does all this for us.

These two shall 'follow' me. The Hebrew term is *Battle Hate.*[5] David had known something of battle hate, being a warrior. He had faced Goliath who had defied the God of the armies of Israel. He had wrestled with many a soldier, seeking to take a city. There was tremendous power and hate in 'battle hate'. All his powers were given over to fighting. With God, what is described as hate is love. As one soldier hated and had to overcome the other, God in love overcomes us, following us, chasing us, seeking after us all the days of our lives. He follows longer and further than the Magi who travelled far and asked 'Where is He?' God, in grace, chases us as a bee going to a flower. It is the suggestion of the strongest possible feeling that God has towards His people. John 3:16 is a large love, but it has to be broken into small portions so that the individual might know it for himself. Surely only goodness and mercy shall tread behind me. That is care. That is comforting. That is caring. That is Christ.

A lady who had had many operations, always used to repeat Psalm 23 before going into the operating theatre. She would stop when she came to the words 'goodness and mercy shall follow me all the days of my life'. The goodness and mercy went with her into and through the operation and were a source of great strength and comfort to her. The goodness and mercy of God held her hands whilst she was operated on.

Wherever we are and wherever we go, the call to goodness, which comes through repentance, and the call of mercy, which bends to every situation, will follow us – all the days of all our lives.

Thirteen

I Will Dwell in The House of The Lord For Ever

Home, Sweet Home

There are many connotations to the word 'house'. There is that which refers to a family, to a tribe, to a nation and to a country. I think the writer has in mind the immediate Presence of God and then, in the future, to dwell in Heaven for ever. To the sheep it meant the next pasture was provided for its benefit and no doubt it would be the best. It was the greener grass on the other side! I love those words 'I will dwell in my Father's heart for ever; He will dwell in my heart for evermore'.

Goodness and mercy have done a thorough work. They have brought us there. Their ministries are now complete in that City. They have helped me to complete my course. Paul had kept the faith (2 Tim. 4:7) because the faith had kept him! Our goal is God Himself. This psalm is an unfinished symphony. It never comes to a full stop and Eternal life in God never does. I will dwell in the Presence and be guided by the persuasion of God for ever. What is here and now, clothed with limitations and shrouded in clouded vision will be there and then unlimited. Grass the greenest it has ever been. There will be no thorny hedges. The only avalanche the sheep will ever know in the House of the Lord is an avalanche of the love of God which will come to the sheep throughout all Eternity. We shall find ourselves fully expressing all that which new nature and new life means in all its abundance in the love of God. Free to roam, free to come and go, free to frolic, kick and skip. The sound of the singing of the birds will have come. The first springtime of Heaven will be ours. Eternal youth with all its yearnings will be fully satisfied. There will be no hidden caves in Heaven, only golden crowns. If the Lord is my Shepherd then Heaven will be a full and final display of His Lordship. He will be truly Lord over all.

Here on earth we have known the limited presence of God, but in the Father's House the limited will become the limitless, it will be the universal. We shall see His Face. We shall meet with the One Who has supplied all things.

The psalm begins with the Lord and it concludes with the for-everness of God's character. When we are in God we look forward to Eternity and all that means. It is purer, greener, sweeter, fuller, higher. The paths of righteousness all converge in God. They are endless in the House of His Presence, even as down here they have been righteous. The green grass and the streams with the table and the overflowing cup have been something down here, but wait until we arrive up there! What a difference! No stream will run dry and the cup will overflow for ever and ever. We shall be led from fountain to fountain. That is some measure when it is measured by the Eternity of God's Nature. We shall not have to move on any more. Permanent and stable satisfaction will be ours. We shall have the sameness, not a sameness of boredom but of variety.

'In My Father's House are many rooms' (John 14:2). What we have dwelt in on earth will be enlarged into something much greater in Heaven. Every pasture has sufficient space for every sheep, whether it be strong or weak, bold or bent, and there will be sufficient space for such in the Father's House. Harps and angels will take the place of lion and bear. There will be no need to shelter during the time of storm, for Jesus has said 'Peace, be still!' It will be a permanent peace, a permanent calmness. That which troubled, such as the roaring of the sea, will be turned into glass. The Rock, Christ Jesus, will be there, instead of the ragged rock. The dim light of the shepherd at night and the dim vision of the sheep, will be removed for ever. The Lamb will be the Light. The Eternity of God is the only chasm which has to be bridged.

There are many negatives in Heaven! No night, no fear, no sorrow, no death, no tears. 'God shall wipe away all tears from their eyes' (Revelation 7:17 & 21:4). It is where God is All in All. It is where He reigns supreme, where Lordship and Sovereignty are the endless order of the endless day. That presence of God which is within us and around us is, by the Spirit of God, preparing us for Father's immediate Presence in Eternity.

The attacks on the sheep will be ended. The sleepless nights will be no more. The sheep will not be used as sleeping pills! The hard and the barren will be no more. The valley of the shadow of death has been turned upside down into a glorious mountain of testimony to the grace of God which has brought us through. As I have been at home in this mortal body, so I shall be perfectly at home in a new body in the Presence of the Father (2 Corinthians 5:8 & 9). If God is going to present us with a new body at the Rapture (1 Thessalonians 4:16 & 17; 1 Corinthians 15:35–45), that body will need a floor to walk on and a place to live in. Heaven will be the perfect environment for the new body. There will be no pollution in Heaven. We shall receive lips to taste, eyes to see, feet to walk. There will be an appreciation of what God has prepared for those who love Him. We only have the engagement ring, the pledge of paradise here. Jesus said, 'I go to prepare a place for you'. The Greek word TOPOS is the word from which we receive our word 'topic' and also 'topography', map drawing and land contour design, the describing of a place. In the New Testament it describes the real places which are akin to the House of the Lord. It is used of a region and a locality. It defines a home and the contents of that home (Luke 2:7 & 14:22) – describing a room. It depicts a place which a thing occupies, couch, table, chair (Luke 14:9 & 10).[6]

As the sword rests in the scabbard, we shall rest in the presence of God, our home. In the New Testament the same word found in John 14:2 and Luke 11:33 describes a place for a candle; John 19:17 describes the place where they crucified Jesus, Golgotha. These are all real visible vital places. As things fit into places made for them, so we shall fit into Heaven in the place made for us. God is preparing us whilst we are here on earth. Every bend we travel round is part of the moulding process, the turning of the lathe. God is forming us and framing us, taking us and making us. He is preparing us as we drink from the cup, as we come to the table, as we pass through the valley of the shadow of death.

Remember that when Jesus spoke the words in John 14:2, they had travelled a long way and there was no place, no accommodation for them. Jesus is saying, in effect, 'In My Father's House it will not be like that. There is room for all. Not made out of the boughs and branches of trees'. There is a permanence about the Father's place. Your place is there. We all have likes and dislikes, but what God has prepared for those who love Him will fit into all our desires. It will be so good that it will be perfect for our every need and requirement. We shall say with the Disciples, 'Lord, it is good for us to be here'.

Milk for babies, and meat for men! Heaven will be according to tastes. Heaven will be tastefully decorated with Divine doings. The Father's House will be for the Father's sheep. It will suit everyone. The position we are to occupy will present no problems because it will be according to the pattern of God's plan and will be in His Presence. The experiences of earth will be continued in a perfect manner, eating perfect Manna in Heaven. Those influences of the shepherd with the sheep on earth will be transferred into a higher realm. All the pleasures of Psalm 23 will become the pleasures which are at the right hand of the Father for evermore. In the Father's House are many mansions and all the mansions of earth are not the same. Many are built to certain specifications. Jesus will lay the foundations and the fabrics according to what your feelings are, what your design is and what your delectation requires! The influence of God will not be less, but more.

God will deal with perfect sheep in a perfect manner in a perfect place! The first order and the last order of Heaven is perfection. Buckingham Palace has 602 bedrooms, but what are these when compared with the many mansions for the many sheep?

There is just something about the Shepherd that will never let me leave Him and He will never leave me. With His influence and His ministries He will see me through time and on into Eternity. The grass will be greener, the streams will be wider, the table will accommodate far more, the cup will be larger and nothing will be lost in that which floods over the sides.

One thing will be missing in the House of the Father, and that will be the Valley of the Shadow of Death, for there will be no death (Revelation 21:4). The grass will not brown and the leaf will not wither. The fear and dread of the sheep will be annihilated at His feet. 'I will dwell in the Presence of the Lord for ever'. Wherever the sheep have been there has been no permanence, every scene has been a changing one. The scents of the valleys and hills soon blew away but Heaven's scenery is for ever. Happiness, plesantness and joyfulness will become a forever thing. Every hill, every valley and stream has all been in the changing scenes of time. When we arrive in Heaven we are at Home! Home, sweet home! Paul speaks of it as arriving home (2 Corinthians 5:6 & 8) – as if, on this earth, we have been away from home as pilgrims and strangers, as those just passing through. When we are present at Home with the Lord it means that we have reached the end of the journey on earth and begin a journey which is endless in Heaven. Earth, as with the sheep travelling along, has been a training for reigning! – paths for the purposes of God to be permanent. We shall have the journey but without the tiredness of it (Revelation 14:13).

Heaven will be a lot of things to a lot of people. It will be the crowning of every joy and the light without measure for all who come to the house of the Lord. Most come to a house and go from it for different reasons, but to this House we come for ever. Once we are there it will be so delightful that we shall not want to move or wander off into distant hills. The earthly shepherd will be made redundant! He can hang up both rod and staff.

To the weary, dwelling in the House of the Father will mean rest. To the sickly it will mean health. To the blind it will mean sight. It will be a relief for the tormented. To the hungry, food. To the sad, joy. To the frustrated with great visions it will mean freedom and visions fulfilled. Pain will be a thing of the past. To those who are bedridden it will mean freedom to rest in the love of the Lord. To the saved – full salvation! The servant will receive a full reward. There will be that entering into the joy of the Lord. You will realise that you were made for this, even as the Sabbath Day was made for man (Mark 2:27). All the toils and the paths with the fears and the frights will be worth it. Heaven will not be a race begun but a race won. Not the starter's gun but the Lord's 'Well done'. Death will be the last step as we press towards the mark for the prize. The shadow was leading to the substance and the water which ran away was leading to fountains of everlasting water. The cup which was always having to be refilled is replaced.

I remember returning from Australia in the 1960s and a pretty 15-year-old came to the place where I was staying. She took one look at me and said, 'Well, I am disappointed!' Someone had been extolling looks which I did not possess, and sight had removed the deception! We shall not be disappointed with our appointed place in the House of the Lord. All the pastures and sunny days with fresh flowing water will be placed into one area, Heaven.

The sheep as they travel see through a glass darkly. They are short-sighted and look at many things as through a muddy pool. Paul refers to looking through a glass darkly, through a riddle (1 Corinthians 13:12). Anticipation and speculation will give way to realisation. There, all knowledge will be complete. The things that the sheep do not and could not understand, will be made known. All the knotty problems will be solved. Tongues which tire will cease. There will be endless praise. Knowledge and Prophecy, which are in part, are lost in the wholeness of Heaven and the oneness of wonder. We have all walked by faith, but now we shall see by sight (1 Corinthians 13:9–12).

I remember as a child going home to ask my parents when I didn't understand certain things. I thought my father knew everything! My son, as a small child, often would say to his mother, 'My father will know the answer!'

There will be sheep in Heaven from all dispensations. The men of quality and quest like Noah, Abraham, Enoch, Peter, Paul, and myriads of others have arrived! Heaven will not mark them out as earth's feeble eyes did. You have heard sermons on Jonah and the Whale, but wait until you hear what Jonah has to say! Peter walking on the water – wait until Peter tells the story! The march around Jericho? Preachers have certainly had us falling along with the walls and blowing with the trumpets, marching with the priest; wait until Joshua tells his story!

The Ideal Homes Exhibition will seem so ordinary, despite its modern innovations it will be outdated and outmoded at our first glimpse of the mansion in Heaven! What the believer receives will always be in fashion, it will never be outdated or have a sell-by date!

The shepherd always went before the sheep. Jesus Christ is spoken of as a 'forerunner' (Hebrews 6:20), this word being the one used to describe the Macedonian troops which always went before the main party. A little ship was also called the 'forerunner'. It came out to take the anchor from the main ship and then bring it to port. The main ship was then drawn in. Jesus as Shepherd is our Forerunner. He tasted death for every man (Hebrews 2:9), and He has tasted Heaven for us to make sure it is to our liking. The word 'tasting' in 'tasting death' (Hebrews 2:9) is the same as that used for tasting water turned to wine in John 2:9.

There are those who would want to lift the slabs of the golden streets of Heaven, while others may feel they would like to scrape the pearls off the gates. Some will be happy with kissing the Throne on which the Lamb is seated. There are people who would like to hear angels sing, to see the wings – are they as strong as we think? It is the Shepherd and His Presence only which satisfies the sheep. That which they have passed through on earth would have been dull and incomplete without the presence of the Shepherd. My joy shall be His face to see. To see Him for myself, and not another. There is a saying: See Naples and die! See Jesus and Live!

I was once standing at the school gates and heard the piercing, sobbing cry of a child. I hurried to find out what abnormal thing had happened to cause it. The child was sobbing, 'Mummy, Mummy, you said you would be here!' You can be lonely in a crowd. God your Friend, Jesus Christ your Saviour, will be there! All the saints of all the Ages will be there, but best of all, You can be there as you trust Jesus for your salvation. God will be the full stop which leads to the next paragraph!

The greatest thing in my Father's House is Jesus Christ. 'They shall see His Face' (Revelation 22:4). The glory of Heaven, the Light of Heaven, the Lamb of Heaven, the Music of Heaven, the Laughter and the Joy of Heaven is Jesus Christ.

To be absent from the body and to be at home with the Lord. That is the House of the Lord where I desire to dwell for ever. Not as a static piece of furniture, but as a loving, thinking, moving, appreciating Heavenly Being, entering into the Joy of my Lord. I don't want to be a palm leaf or a harp. I want to be me, fully made, fully developed and finding my own place in Eternity. I may feel I am but a sheep here, of no consequence at all, merely as a speck of dusk or a fly on a twig. God wants to take rats from the rat race and transform them into sheep. Those sheep will be of consequence in the Presence of Christ.

What the shepherds of earth provide for their sheep in wells of water and full cups, in immeasurable stilled waters and tender grasses – there will be the reality of all these in Heaven. If the earthly shepherd did so well for his sheep, then how much greater will be that which the Great Shepherd of the sheep accomplishes for us who are following Him, having no continuing city but seeking one to come whose Builder and Maker is God? (Hebrews 11:10 & 12:22).

On earth we have returned to the Shepherd and Bishop of our souls. In Heaven we return as pilgrims and foreigners. Pilgrims who have found a dwelling place and strangers who have found recognition, who will be known. Pilgrims will not pass through Heaven; there will be no strangers, no foes, only friends.

There may be a picture in this psalm of the Levite who has come from his tent and gone into the Tabernacle, but who then enters the Temple built by Solomon, to dwell there for ever. To him, that is where the Presence of God is. It was a permanence after the dwelling in a tent.

Where Jesus is, that is Heaven. Where Jesus is not, that is hell. Heaven will be the fullest expression of the life of God, without the corruption of earth. It will be a full display of Glory and the crowning of all that has been of God.

'I shall dwell in the House of the Lord, for ever'. Home, Sweet Home!

References

1. Robert Young (1989) *Analytical Concordance to the Bible*, Lutterworth Press, Cambridge, England.
2. Campbell Morgan. *Exposition of the Whole Bible*, pp 221. Pickering and Inglis, London.
3. William Barclay (1969) *The Daily Study Bible*, p 194–5 (*Gospel of John*). The Saint Andrew Press, Edinburgh, Scotland.
4. James Strong (1977) *Exhaustive Concordance*. Baker Book House, Grand Rapids, Michigan, America.
5. James Hastings (1925) *The Speaker's Bible*, Vol 7, page 147. (A quotation from J.E. McFaden's *The Divine Pursuit*, p. 201)
6. *Vine's Expository Dictionary of Biblical Words*. Thomas Nelson, Camden, New York.

Additional References

Reference is also made in this book, to John Bunyan's *Pilgrim's Progress* (pp. 26, 54, 59 & 102), Daniel Defoe's *Robinson Crusoe* (p. 53) and Matthew Henry's *Commentary on the Psalms* (p. 62).

The King James version of the bible has been used, unless otherwise stated.